A Wide Woman on a Narrow Boat

Stephanie Green

Published in 2016 by FeedARead.com Publishing

A CIP catalogue record for this title is available from the British Library.

Dedicated to:

Michael Ledger

1946 - 2014

Looking at Boats

My daughter came to Cambridge for the weekend and decided that she would meet up with both of her parents for dinner, despite the fact that the said parents had been divorced for seventeen years and were not always on the best of terms. After all what was the point of seeing each of us separately when she could make do with one evening of filial duty and see us both together? That would give her more time during the rest of her stay for meeting up with old school friends, partying and getting drunk. I started to raise objections but she told me in no uncertain terms that she was sure both of us could tolerate spending a short time together in the same room for the sake of their beloved daughter. The relationship between the ex and myself, which varied from glacial to murderously hot, was at a lukewarm stage so maybe we could manage an evening of food, wine and polite conversation without either of us having to check the sharpness of the knives.

The atmosphere throughout dinner remained harmonious and afterwards, as it was a warm evening, we all decided to stroll along the riverbank to have a drink in The Fort St George. Both the ex and I stopped to peer into a narrow boat moored alongside the bank.

'I'm thinking of selling the house and living on one of these.' I told him.

'Are you?' he said. 'So am I.'

It transpired that for totally different reasons we had both decided that this was going to be our new way of life. I was thinking of buying a beautiful boat and

5

sailing off into the sunset spending my spare time writing the best-selling novel. He was going to buy a beautiful boat and sail off into the sunset and paint glorious pictures. If it was geographically possible on this small island it would be best, for the sanity of both of us, if we headed for different sunsets.

Many a time I have wondered what made us get married all those years ago, now I realised that it was a penchant for having totally stupid, impractical ideas. Neither of us had been on a narrow boat before and had no idea what it entailed but that didn't stop us from being sure it would provide us with the perfect lifestyle.

In the gathering dusk of a mild spring evening we moved along the line of moored boats peering into windows and muttering words like freedom and travel, idyllic and relaxing, friendly and community, alternative and eco-friendly and cheap. Cheap was a word that often cropped up but we never used the words ignorance or bliss.

I have to admit that I was niggled by his decision to live on a boat just at the time I had thought of doing so. I was aware that he knew nothing of my half formulated plans to change my lifestyle but at the same time I felt he was copying me. I wanted mine to be a unique decision, surprising friends, family and acquaintances, and now there were two of us doing it would just appear commonplace. But I attempted to put these thoughts aside and we kept in touch and were lulled into a feeling of compatibility because of our sudden interest in narrow boats and canals and laid-back, idyllic life-styles.

A few weeks later we decided we would go together to look at some narrow boats that were advertised for sale. My sister, Marcelle, was staying with me so she came along for the ride. It proved to be a bumpy ride. The ex was driving, I was map reading, sister sat quietly in the back. If it had taken a pleasant wine-filled evening and a new interest in boats to make me think about why we got married, it only took ten minutes of being together in the same car to remind me of why we got divorced. The multitude of roundabouts afflicting Northampton combined with my general uselessness at map reading and my inability to tell my left from my right ignited his short fuse. So he shouted and drove too fast and I said, 'Right, no not that right the right on this side of the road,' and he drove faster and got in the wrong lane and we went round most roundabouts twice and sometimes came back to them for another try at getting in the wrong lane and once again to turn right when I actually meant that we should have turned left.

When we did locate the boatyards our bad tempers had become entrenched and we grumpily tramped amongst the boats, climbed in and poked around and snapped at each other.

Trying to ignore him and focus on the task in hand, I started to get a pattern of why the boats were differently priced. I eliminated features I didn't want; noted things I liked.

I decided in favour of windows, rather than portholes, because I wanted lots of light. I wanted a cruiser stern not a trad stern. Trad sterns only have room for the person doing the steering but cruiser sterns have more room for many people and I envisaged cruising along on cloudless summer days with a group of friends, all of us sipping chilled wine or fruit laden Pimms, chatting and laughing, while I gently steered the boat through peaceful countryside.

I preferred layouts with the dining area and sitting area together because it made small boats seem more spacious and I developed a hatred of cratch covers (the canopy over the seating area at the front of the boat) because I felt they made the interior of the boat dark.

In the interim, between peering into boats on Midsummer Common and this expedition to boatyards, I had read boating books and magazines and realised I really should do what they advised: spend some time on a boat before deciding to buy one; research boat builders and fitters thoroughly; learn about the mechanical type thingies. The more I'd read about narrow boats and canals the more I was aware of how little I knew. Walking around the marinas, climbing on and off boats, sometimes with great difficulty because I hadn't yet got the hang of negotiating tight turns and narrow entrances, and being baffled by the specifications convinced me I needed to give a lot more thought to the whole business of living on boats before I decided if this was to be my new way of life.

It was late afternoon when we arrived at Braunston Marina, the last boatyard on our itinerary. It was starting to rain, the light was drab and the marina was crowded and dreary. The ex had stopped being bad tempered and had reverted to sulking because at the previous marina he'd found his perfect boat but he couldn't put down a holding deposit until his money was available. He was convinced the boat would be sold before he could buy it. My sister was tired and fed-up with us bitching at each other and was wondering why she hadn't stayed at home to read her book. I was just fed-up of boats, marinas and life in general. We decided we would look at one more boat, then drive home and thankfully go our separate ways. I was reading the specifications and decided I wasn't even going to bother looking at this boat: the dining area was in the wrong place, it had too many portholes, it was too long, it had a cratch cover and a trad stern and I'd decided against all of those. The ex was already grumbling his way aboard so I reluctantly started to follow. He put his hand on a table propped up in the bow, it collapsed and he was catapulted across the bow, smashed his knee against the gunwale and almost went into the water at the other side. He lay in the bow clutching his knee while ranting and raving at the stupidity of idiots who left unstable tables about. He screeched that this was the worst designed boat he'd ever seen.

My sister and I stepped over his prone, groaning, body and went into the boat. 'I don't like this one' she said, 'it's too dark.' and she turned on her heel and left

I stood there and looked through the door. It looked OK to me. I turned around. The ex was still lying there moaning dramatically. This boat had obviously inflicted a grievous injury and caused him serious pain.

So I bought her.

Buying the Boat

I went back into the marina and said, 'I want to buy Rea.' When we had taken the keys for the boat the man in the office at Braunston Marina had been as irritable as the ex and as gloomy as the weather. Not being in the best of moods myself I'd almost thrown the boat keys back at him and made various suggestions as to where he could stuff all his narrow boats: one by one. Now at the sound of the words, 'I want to buy Rea,' he miraculously changed from a lugubrious Eeyore into a bouncy Tigger. His gloom lifted, his face brightened, he sat me down and offered me coffee. He enthused about the craftsmanship of the Merlin fit-out and the reliability of Barrus engines and the swim of Reeves hulls. I sat there attempting to adopt the demeanour of a knowledgeable woman with good taste who recognised a quality boat when she saw one. He asked me if I'd like to take the boat, 'for a spin,' so I could try her out and see how she handled. Looking out of the window at the relentless drizzle and at the sixty foot length of my potential boat I told him that unfortunately, as much as I'd like to have the opportunity to drive her I didn't have time for a spin. One minute on that boat trying to distinguish the steering end from the pointy bit at the front would have stripped away the thin veneer of discerning boat buyer and shown me up for the boating ignoramus that I actually was. I might have tried to admire her wonderful swim (shouldn't boats float not swim?) but in reality I wouldn't know if she was handling like a finely honed, expensively designed ocean going yacht or a leaky old bath tub adrift in the Atlantic.

The enthusiasm of the expert convinced me I was making the right decision and that this was a boat worth the asking price. I assumed it was the boat he was enthusiastic about and not the prospect of a nice wodge of commission on the completion of the sale but I could have been wrong, my daughter is always telling me that they have removed the word gullible from the dictionary.

So I left a deposit and arranged for a marine survey and went back to the car where my sister was huddled on the back seat reading and the ex was rubbing his leg, flinching and definitely not talking to me. I'd found my perfect boat and having already sold my house I had the wherewithal to pay for it while he'd found his perfect boat, Melanie, but had to wait for the completion of his house sale before it was sensible to put a deposit down. So we drove back towards Cambridge to the accompaniment of his moans and groans and ouches every time he had to change gear. The sounds of his pain were interspersed with the phrases 'It's all right for you.', 'Melanie will be sold before I can put a deposit down.', 'You always have all the luck.' 'IT'S NOT FAIR.' I kept quiet and eventually we got home and went our separate ways vowing never, ever, to meet up again.

Rea passed her inspection with more or less a clean bill of health and two weeks later I went back to Braunston to take possession of her. Buying a boat is easier than buying a house, probably easier than buying a car for there is very little in the way of paper work, registration or legislation. I wrote a cheque and I owned a boat and in the process I'd also acquired a new home and a new way of life.

F.A.Qs

'What do you do about receiving your post?' Don't know.

'How do you register with a doctor? errrrrr.....

'What happens if you are in the middle of nowhere and you have an accident?' I don't intend to have any accidents.

'Won't you be nervous, all alone and moored on an isolated tow path at night?' Of course I won't be nervous.

'What happens to her poo?' a friend's eight year old daughter asks him. 'I don't know,' he tells her 'it must go into the river.' 'Uggghhh that's disgusting.' she says, 'I'm never going to eat fish again.' Actually, I tell him it goes into a holding tank under my bed. He's less impressed by that information than his daughter was by his inaccurate information, 'So you spend the night sleeping on top of your poo, ugghh that's even more disgusting. I prefer to think of it going in the river and feeding the fishes.'

'What made you decide to live in a corridor on a drain?' another friend asks. I can see his point. Narrow boats are narrow, the clue lies in the name. They are only 6ft 10ins wide and that includes the steel walls, the padding and the cladding. I am learning to walk like a crab because I am wider than the passageway. I have bruises on my hips where I've walked into a knob that holds the table upright and bruises on my arm where I

keep catching the brass rails that hold the bottom of the curtains in place. Narrow boats are low as well as narrow. I have permanent concussion because I forget to duck when I come in through the low front door. The boat is moored in a marina amidst hundreds of other boats and I'm so close to the boat next to me that if we opened our bathroom windows at the same time each morning we could clean each other's teeth. What's more the canal outside the marina could hardly be described as a fast flowing, burbling stream, a ditch is a more apt description for that murky stretch of water. He could be right about living in a corridor on a drain.

But the most frequently asked question of the frequently asked questions is, *'Are you Living the Dream?'* It is many people's dream to buy a narrow boat, live on board and cruise the canals and waterways of England. There even seem to be an inordinate number of boats called, 'Living the Dream.' It has never been my dream. Until recently it was not a scenario that had even entered my head. The truth is that it just seemed a good idea at the time. That time being when my friend Jessica and I were sauntering along the banks of the Great Ouse on a hot summer's day and we stopped to chat with two men drinking wine and sunning themselves on the roof of a boat. We were invited on board to look around and we were asked if we would like to join them for a cruise down to the pub at the conflagration of the Great Ouse and the Old West River. We didn't go on board to look around or go on the cruise to the pub but the idea of floating down to a pub on a hot summer's afternoon seemed very tempting. Since then the skies have clouded over and the pub they were about to visit has fallen into the river. But just to say blithely, 'Oh, it just seemed like a good idea,' when I've made a huge life-changing decision is a bit feeble. It makes friends and family head home and Google Alzheimer's and watch me closely for signs of senile dementia. I quickly learn when I'm asked if I'm, 'Living the Dream' to find a less airy fairy, pie in the sky response. I usually reply, 'No, I'm Living the Financial Necessity'. Then, at least, I get nods of sympathy and understanding instead of advice to go and see a psychiatrist immediately.

There is some truth about 'Living the Financial Necessity'. When the Credit Crunch hit and work started to dry up it was sensible to get rid of the mortgage. I did think that mortgage free I could invest some of the equity from the house and also buy a boat. Then I would cruise around England, eat frugally and live a simple life. Never again would I have to face a pre-dawn morning on the M25 just to get to a job to earn not quite enough money to pay the bills. Yet I am beginning to realise that living on a boat is not going to be as economical as I first anticipated. I will have to pay for a licence that allows me to be on the canals and rivers, mooring fees, insurance, a safety certificate, maintenance, diesel, gas and pints of cider in the local pubs. The cost of living on a boat is likely to be higher than I imagined. I didn't do any detailed sums, I just had a vague, plucked from the air, idea about how much it would cost to run a boat and how much I would need to live on. I think I needed to have plucked a few more figures from the air.

I could, of course, have bought a smaller house taken in a lodger and got a job. But that was being sensible and I didn't feel this was the time to be sensible. After all you're only old once.

Maybe the main reason for the decision to live on a boat was that I was simply feeling restless. I'd recently returned from a two year stint with VSO in the Philippines working with women's groups. I was finding the return difficult. When I'd left I had thrown out years of accumulated possessions, mostly old tat, and now I was back I didn't want to re-fill a house with more old tat and I was determined not to slip back into my old way of life. I had spent two years living with very few belongings, with running water which only ran between midnight and 5am and an eccentric electricity supply. Perhaps deciding to live within the narrow confines of the boat with a need to fill a water tank and carry coal and gas was an attempt to re-create this more basic life-style. Perhaps I thought moving to the canals was a way of recreating the excitement of moving to a foreign land but a foreign land where I spoke the language and where I would be relatively near my children and would be able to pop over to see friends if I got lonely. For I had loved the Philippines and the Filipinos but I had become lonely and I had my missed my children very much and I'd missed my friends and I'd missed cheese.

In those first few weeks on board my new boat I had no regrets about my half-baked decision to buy her. When I woke up in the morning the reflections of the sun on the water made golden porthole shaped shimmies on the panelling and enhanced the texture of the wood. When the sun warmed the boat it started to creak and grumble into life and when I got out of bed the floor swayed gently as I walked along it. I decided I loved my boat. Admittedly this was a honeymoon period in beautiful late August sunshine when I wasn't going anywhere, just sitting there doing a bit of brass polishing and cleaning and getting used to a new environment. I hadn't had the chance to get lonely, feel isolated or have problems with temperamental engines, dodgy batteries or leaks in the plumbing. I was vaguely aware that when I ventured out into the turbulence and cut and thrust of the Grand Union Canal life might be a bit different, a bit more uncertain, a bit more tense. And I'd be all by myself. I try not to think that it could all turn into 'Living the Nightmare'.

I had bought a sixty-foot boat with lots of portholes, a traditional stern, a dining area separate from the lounge and the dreaded cratch cover, which I am still determined to get rid of. Not the specifications I'd been intending to live with but then you don't always fall in love with the perfect man let alone the perfect boat. I most certainly didn't intend to buy a boat quite so long. I'd calculated that fifty feet was long enough to provide enough living space and be manageable out on the water. I certainly didn't want anything more than fifty five feet because that would be too long to navigate some of the northern canals. Never mind with two thousand miles of canals to choose from I can probably exist happily without visiting the Huddersfield Broad

Canal. From the inside sixty foot of boat still seems short and cramped but from the outside it seems endless.

I had expected in a blasé sort of way that I wouldn't find it a problem handling the sailing (do you sail a narrow boat?) single-handed and doing the locks by myself and if there were a lot of locks to do then I would have plenty of willing crew members to come on board and help. I've now walked along the canal bank and looked at those locks and they do seem deep and the ladders to get out are green and slimy and to operate them by myself I would have to be able to climb onto the roof to walk to the ladders to get out. I've tried operating the locks and the mechanisms are stiff and the lock gates heavy. I've looked at the canal outside Braunston and it's crowded and narrow. I'm beginning to realise that doing it all alone may not be an easy task. I may need help. But all my potential help has disappeared over the horizon. All my prospective crew members appear to have prior appointments, jobs to go to, gardens to tend, sick grannies to visit and one has even acquired a dog which won't get in a car so that makes it absolutely impossible for her to visit.

I've also talked to a few boaters in the vicinity and seen their reaction when I tell them that I'm planning to live on and move this thing around by myself. The women invariably say, 'Aren't you brave.' The men raise their eyebrows in a, 'She'll never remember to tighten the stern gland,' sort of way.

When the list of frequently asked but unanswerable questions is exhausted there is a pause, followed by the statement, 'You must meet lots of interesting people on the canals.' Who do they think meanders along these two thousand miles of stagnant water? Poets and philosophers, rock stars and international criminals, party animals and raconteurs. What is an interesting person? One man's interesting person is the next man's pub bore. I don't think the statement, 'You must meet lots of interesting people on the caravan sites,' crops up very often. But after a week's immersion in the world of narrow boats I am coming to the conclusion that narrow boating is just caravanning without the wheels.

There are boating stereotypes. Yachting has its Simon and Caroline in yellow wellies, red faced and salt encrusted from battling gales on the high seas and from imbibing a surfeit of gin. After a short time in a marina I decide the narrow boating stereotype is Brian and Janet, wearing comfy trainers and looking forward to a nice cup of tea at the end of a hard day chugging along sluggish water at four miles an hour. There's not a lot of battling against the elements on the canals although I've heard that there's a lock at Brampton that can be a bit tricky when the wind's from the east.

Brian and Janet have taken early retirement and they actually are, 'Living the Dream'. Brian is paunchy, sports a beard, does the driving and spends his spare time in long and intense conversations with the other Brians about engines and gearboxes. Janet is fit and wiry, wears baggy, beige shorts which expose legs where stringy muscles do battle with her varicose veins. She works the locks and polishes the brass work. When Brian is relaxing with the Daily Mail after a tiring day at the tiller she cooks nourishing stews or, if the weather is warm, arranges colourful salads. They pride themselves on working as an efficient team. The predominant hair colour is grey and ethnic minorities are conspicuous by their absence.

Now, in late summer, it's getting near the time when Brian and Janet will move the geraniums from the roof of the boat and take them back to their bungalow in Nuneaton where they'll spend the winter gazing at waterway maps and planning next season's boating. Or next season's adventures as they like to refer to their travels through Middle England. 'Adventures', sound to me as if they are setting off down the Amazon in a small canoe instead of pottering along in a solid steel hull in water that is only four feet deep.

In the interests of research I have bought a book in a charity shop about cruising on the waterways, it was first published in the 1960s. It says, 'Remember that steering a boat may be a wonderful change from work for you but cooking and washing up on a boat isn't much of a change for your wife,' and, 'Don't assume because your wife can't drive the family car she isn't able to handle a boat.' (The author always addresses the male reader so he must assume that women are incapable of reading a book as well as being incapable of driving the family car.) It is a statement that would never appear in books that have been published in the last thirty years, yet with my brief observations of life as it is lived on the canals I think the sentiment of, 'Men drive – women cook,' still holds true for many boaters. There seems to be a lower percentage of

20

female boat handlers than there are women in David Cameron's cabinet.

I'm spending a lot of time fraternising with the Brians and Janets. I quickly get bored with cleaning and polishing so I'm very happy to stop for a chat and listen to tales of derring-do on the canals, or the Cut as us seasoned boaters call it. Only the more I listen and learn the more I wonder if I'm suited to this slower pace of life.

'Five days to reach Oxford?' I could walk there in half the time.

'Slow down to two miles an hour to pass moored boats?' For Christ's sake if they chose to live on a boat the occupants must expect a bit of turbulence.

'Three hours to get along that piddling little stretch of water?' Can't you just put your foot on the accelerator?'

I've also been reading the boaters blogs. There are a lot of them, mostly detailing journeys along stretches of canal, miles from where I'm moored and which I didn't even know existed, so I've confined myself to reading the ones who are travelling in this area or are ranting about the misbehaviour of other boaters. I do enjoy reading a good rant.

There is a boat blogger's terminology. They are always stopping for a 'natter' with other boaters, they insist all conversations between boaters include the subjects of toilets and when they set off anywhere they are going to have those adventures.

I read that Ken and Margaret have stopped in Rugby and managed to get a new pair of glasses for Ken.

21

Graham and Elaine have had problems with a slow moving boat and it took them three hours to get down the Napton Flight. I'm already discovering that all boaters proclaim the wonders of the slow pace of life but get very angry when a dilatory boat in front slows it down even further.

In Braunston itself Brian and Janet have had a huge disappointment. They had planned on having an ice-cream to reward them for their hard work down the locks of the Braunston Flight, but when they got there the shop was closed.

Am I going to fit in here? Am I going to be able to cope with all these new adventures? Will the excitement be too much for me?

I might not have been living a life that could have been defined as, 'fast' but, even so, I seem to have gone from eighty miles an hour to four miles an hour in the time it takes to sign a cheque for forty two thousand pounds. I wanted to get away from the M25, to stop hurtling suicidally along the outside lane because yet again I was late for an appointment. But am I temperamentally suited to life in the slow lane? Do I have the patience to travel through England at snail's pace? Given a long straight stretch of canal will I be overcome with the urge to put my foot down and hurtle along at six miles an hour, destroying banksides and ducks nests with my wash, rocking moored boats and gaining a reputation as an inconsiderate boater?

Lessons

Driving a boat must be easy, that little pin man in my boaters' manual doesn't seem to have any problems. If he can do it then I can do it. I've read The Boater's Handbook from cover to cover. I've got a Waterways Manual and any number of leaflets and sets of instructions. I've watched the video, 'Learning to Handle a Narrow Boat,' on the Waterscape website. The video features two families going on holiday. One is a Goody Two Shoes couple who have read the books and listened to the instructions, the other is a fat family who haven't. You just know which one is going to get it all right and which is going to get it wrong. Sadly I can relate more to the fat family that carry copious amounts of food and beer on board than I can relate to a woman with all the oomph of a librarian on Prozac who says, 'We haven't been on holiday since we got the cats.' The families are asked to designate the skipper of the boat and in both cases the men are chosen. The fat family breaks all the rules and heads off in the wrong direction. The boring couple, apart from a bit of speeding that creates a breaking wash, do everything correctly. In the end it turns out well for both families. The sun shines, everybody has a wonderful time and none of the crew has problems with steering, getting around bends or driving into narrow locks. So it must be easy, if they can do it then I can do it.

The theory might be fine but the reality is rather

more daunting. When I stand at the back, hand experimentally on the tiller, it seems a very long way to the front and the thought of negotiating something of this length frightens me. I do the first sensible thing I've done so far in this narrow boat saga: I book a day's tuition with an experienced boatman.

Then I revert to my usual non-sensible self and invite the ex along for the day. Why? Is it my kind heart having its mothballs dusted off and wanting him to enjoy a day on the boat or am I just being smug because I have my lovely boat and he is still waiting to buy one? He receives strict instructions that he is to be on his best behaviour: he is here to observe only, he is not to take over the day by asking lots of questions. It is my day of training not his and on no account will he be allowed to drive my boat.

There are a lot of instructors on the canals and deciding which instructor is the right one for me could have meant a many hours research and a hefty telephone bill. So being a superficial sort of person I chose the instructor with the prettiest brochure.

The ex turned up early at 7.45am. Martin, the instructor, arrived promptly at 8am and told me as there were two people doing the course instead of one he was charging me double. That got us off to a good start. Martin's hair style was modelled on a sparse toothbrush and he had the ruddy, broken veined complexion of a lifetime spent out in the open air. Or on the booze. Martin is a voluble bloke and managed to impart a lot of information in a short time. He informed me about his days in the Navy, his boat and how he's doing amazingly expert and complicated renovations on it, about his views on the economy, immigration and his failed marriage (I can't understand why she left such a wonderful man). He told me how every other boater on the canals, apart from the odd fellow professional and boaters that had been Martin trained, are at best incompetent and at worst downright dangerous.

Eventually he got down to explaining about how to maintain the boat and move around safely. He gave me a lot of vital information but having already spent nearly an hour listening to the story of his life I'd switched off so I missed most of it.

The ex was behaving himself and sitting quietly listening to all the information without interrupting or asking questions. I hoped he'd absorbed some of Martin's words of wisdom and would be able to pass them onto me later because I definitely hadn't absorbed a thing.

Two mugs of tea and a volume of words later we set off. Martin got us out of the tightly packed marina easily, at the same time expounding his views on the scourge of the hire boaters. These pariahs of the canals do dreadful things like steering into bridges and leaving lock gates open. Evidently, they are all incredibly stupid and a menace to all forms of waterway and tow-path life.

I don't mention it to Martin but I have a great deal of respect for people who hire boats then take them out, family tucked neatly away on board, with only the minimum of instruction. I have a feeling that given enough time and a following wind that I will outdo most of them in the contest for the most incompetent boater.

I do remember a few useful things. I remember him telling me that if you fall in the canal not to get straight into a hot shower because it can precipitate a heart attack. I also learn a mantra that stands me in good stead in the future, 'Point your tiller towards what you want to get away from.'

When he had deftly negotiated us through tight entrances, narrow bridges, moored boats and canal traffic and we reached a straight, quiet, hazard free bit of canal Martin let me steer my boat. To people used to driving cars or riding bikes or horses the tiller on a boat is counter-intuitive, to turn left you push it to the right. I get the hang of it quite quickly and steer round bends and through the bridges and sometimes I almost avoid hitting them. It's when I have to execute an unexpected manoeuvre that I go wrong. When a hazard presents itself, and that hazard is usually another boat, instinct takes control of the brain, remembers I usually drive a car and overrules everything I have been learning about driving a boat. My steering goes to pot and we're veering towards a collision. I forget that a boat doesn't have brakes just a reverse thrust and I throw it into neutral which means I have no steering at all and it's now drifting rapidly towards that collision. Just before the point of impact Martin pushes me out of the way, grabs the tiller and the throttle and expertly gets us out of trouble. As we pass the driver at the helm of the other boat he gives a knowing, eyebrows raised, 'Aged female driver,' look in my direction. I scramble out of the well of the boat, where I have been ignominiously shoved, with as much dignity as I can muster, brush myself down and once again take my place at the tiller.

I am surprised at how heavy the steering is, my arm is soon aching and although we might be going slowly if I take some time to look around and admire the scenery the bow is suddenly embedded in bank or bushes. I'd heard travelling on narrow boats is relaxing; where's the relaxation in this? That's what I want to know.

We trundle along, most of Martin's instructions and words of wisdom passing through one ear and out the other without registering in the brain. I know women are supposed to be able to multi-task but I can't. I never have been able to. How can he expect me to drive a boat and listen to him at the same time? Those pin men in the Boater's Handbook, the prissy couple and the fat man in the video never had to wrestle with the tiller and they didn't keep hitting the banks so why can't I steer it properly? An urgent hooting and flashing of lights from a boat moving away from the bank behind us makes us stop. I panic. Have I hit somebody? The driver just grins and waves, he was putting his coat on and the toggles got caught in the instrument panel. It amuses me but Martin is disgusted and issues another of his instructions, 'Don't wear coats with toggles.'

To complete our stretch, we go through a lock, turn round, come back and stop for lunch. Martin doesn't want to share my French bread, brie, hummus and salad. 'Poncy food,' he says dismissively and devours his own ham sandwiches and cheese and onion crisps instead. The ex tucks in and tells me it is, 'a lovely lunch,' He's obviously remembered the instruction to be on his best behaviour. A hire boat crewed by pirates glides by, most of the pirates are sharing the roof with crates of beer and lager. Martin hops out and trots along the towpath beside them so he can share with them his knowledge of the laws relating to drinking and driving on the inland waterways (I check later: the 2003 Railways and Transport Safety Act sets proposals about alcohol limits, similar to those on the roads, but they haven't been implemented yet). Martin tells me he never drinks when he's in charge of the boat. He tells me this many times during the course of the day. He doth protest too much, methinks.

So we set off again. Martin is talking, I am listening (sometimes) and the ex is standing quietly on the gunwales. When we are almost home we catch up with a boat moving very slowly in front of us; evidently on straight stretches he should move over to let us pass. He doesn't. Martin gets angry and instructs me to move up close to his stern and blow the horn. I refuse. The ex and Martin suddenly discover male bonding and become angry in unison. Martin leans over and blows the horn, long and loud, and the other boat eventually moves over. We overtake. Martin shouts at him. The ex shakes his fist. It's my first experience of canal rage. There's as much anger, shouting and gesticulation as at any motorway incident, only as it happens much more slowly a more complete litany of the guilty boaters misdemeanours and lack of consideration can be expounded by our perfect and perfectly irritating instructor.

Life on the canals is supposedly laid back and I was expecting a much gentler attitude to other boaters. I am tempted to tell them both that this is my boat and they either modify their behaviour or get off. The thought that Martin might do just that and I would have to park this monster in the crowded marina by myself means I only tell the ex to behave or get off. I just frown gently at Martin.

On learning to handle a narrow boat it appears that you also have to learn how to tie it up. Knots are important. You are judged by other narrow boaters, or to be more precise by other male narrow boaters, on the quality of your knots and by the way in which your boat is neatly (or not) tethered to the bank or mooring.

I can't do knots. My sister, on going rock climbing, was complimented on her ability to learn knotting (if that's what it's called). She said, 'I come from a long line of sailors, it's in my blood.' Well I come from that same long line of sailors but my blood runs completely free of any knot tying talent. I have inherited my ancestral sailors love of the sea, their love of boats and their propensity to run to fat but the knot tying gene has completely passed me by.

I've got a book on tying knots and it's got a handy little red rope tied to the front to practice on. I've practised and I've practised. I've done cloves and reefs and boatman's hitch and taut line hitch. I've stood back to admire them and they look wonderful. I give them a tug and they either metamorphose into granny knots and fall apart or solidify into an undoable clump. I was always impressed by the cowboys in films who came running out of the bar with the baddies chasing them, pulled their hitch knot, jumped on the horse and galloped off. If it had been me I'd have pulled at the knot, tightened it instead of loosening it and seconds later I'd lay dead in the dust with fifty bullet holes in me. When I used to ride horses everybody else had their hitches knotted efficiently. After a break they would untie and mount their horses and then wait for me to break all my fingernails, swear and sweat profusely, and take an age to untie the sodding reins. Either that or I'd tie my horse up securely, walk away down the drive and then be aware of clopping hooves behind me and watch perplexed as he trotted passed on his way to greener pastures.

During my narrow boat handling lesson I feel as if I've spent more time fiddling with the ropes than I have spent driving the boat. Rope throwing I did competently once I'd become annoyed enough with Martin to try and decapitate him with the rope instead of just throwing it to him. The knots never worked. In the end Martin gave up and when we arrived back at the marina he tied the boat up himself and disappeared hurriedly into the sunset. The ex disappeared equally as hurriedly in the opposite direction. I went straight to my car to drive to the supermarket to buy copious amounts of alcohol.

On coming out of the supermarket car park and meeting a queue at the exit I tried to brake. My leg wouldn't move to the brake pedal. I tried harder to move it. It was immoveable, paralysed. I grabbed the handbrake, pulled it on and stopped inches from the car in front. I looked at my leg to see why it had suddenly become immobile and saw that my shoe lace had come undone and I'd trapped it in the door, hence not being able to move my foot over to the brake pedal. If, at my age, I can't even tie my shoe-laces properly the chances of learning to do a boatman's hitch which will be the envy of all the other boaters on the canal system are slim. I will simply wrap the ropes tightly around the chains or bollards and hope Rea and I don't drift away during the night.

The Maiden Voyage

My friend Jessica bravely agrees to come with me for my maiden voyage. She can't swim so we visit the local chandlers to buy her a life-jacket. Jessica is the consummate shopper, she likes to look at the products on offer, ask a lot of questions, compare prices and quality and then bargain about the price. My method of shopping, and I only ever enter a shop if I am in dire need of the goods on offer, is to walk in say, 'that will do' and get out as quickly as possible. Shopping together means that she marches into every shop with a grumbling gremlin in tow; occasionally she spits at me, 'It's like shopping with a man.' Eventually I get completely fed-up, buy a newspaper and tell her to meet me in the pub when she's finished. But today is different for two major reasons: I like chandlers, I can poke around them looking at ropes and loops and brassy things for ever. The second reason is that the longer Jessica spends looking at life-jackets the more distant is the time at which I have to get on the back of that bloody long boat and drive it. At the third chandlers another customer tells her if she falls in the canal all she needs to do is put her feet down and walk out. The canals are shallow. So we decide to spend the life-jacket money on a pub lunch and thereby put off the evil hour of setting sail for even longer.

Eventually we leave. I remember advice from Martin to use the wind and I look at which way the marina flag is flying and let the wind take my bow round. I get out of the tight mooring very neatly. ('It was quite good for a girl' the marina owner tells me later.) With the help of Jessica's semaphore signals from the bow I get out of the narrow exit from the marina and onto the canal without any scraping of paintwork against concrete. I feel pleased with myself, relax and promptly prang a moored boat. Everybody says, 'Narrow boating is a contact sport' but they only say that when other boats are hitting each other. When their boat is the one being hit they spring to life snarling, 'Slow down,' 'Be more careful,' 'Look where you're going,' at the perpetrator. I mouth apologies to the irate owner of the boat I've just scraped and we motor on our way.

Gradually I realise I'm enjoying this and I wonder what all that worry and prevarication was about. I didn't buy a boat to sit in a marina and polish the brass work. This was why I bought a boat: to progress steadily through gently rolling countryside on a sunny day with a good friend on board and wine in the fridge. I'm going to like this way of life.

We have decided not to attempt any locks on our first day and slow down to moor along the towpath before Hillmorton Locks. I don't think I slowed down enough, Jessica jumped off with the rope and heaved on it, the man from the boat in front jumped off his boat and came running down the towpath towards us, shouting instructions and grabbing the rope. 'Didn't mean to be officious,' he explained when we were safely stopped and moored, 'but I've got a pan of jam on the stove and it could have been a bit messy if you'd hit me.' Phaaa... he obviously hadn't realised what an expert helmsman I am. I wouldn't have hit him.

When we are moored up securely I go inside. It seems strange. The scenery has passed on by, my location has changed, I've talked to different people but my home is still with me, the bed is there, the chairs haven't moved and the washing up is still in the sink. This never happened with my house, when I went away for the weekend it just stayed where it was. I didn't have to take it with me.

The following morning we set off for the locks. Jessica, pre-trained on our early morning stroll, trotted off ahead windlass in hand ready to do her impersonation of a highly skilled crew member. I started the boat, cast off and stood at the stern, tiller in hand, ready to do my impersonation of a highly skilled helmsman. Hillmorton Locks are parallel single locks with a patch of grass twenty feet wide between each lock basin. 'Which lock?' she shouted. I pointed to the one on the left. When she had the gates almost open I set off, then slowed down to wait for her to complete the operation. Then suddenly the wind or the overflow channel or an act of God appeared from nowhere and took charge of the boat. It wasn't me, I was in perfect control until some alien being or a freak of nature took the boat sideways towards the opposite bank and plastered it against a disused barge.

'Which lock are you using?' shouted a puzzled, lone

34

boater who'd been following along behind me and was intending to go through the lock I wasn't using.

'I wish I knew.' I shouted back, 'You take the open lock and I'll go into the other one.'

'I can't take your water,' he said doubtfully.

'Don't worry about it. I think we'll both find that is the easiest option.'

Jessica finished opening the gates and turned to wave me in. I was behind her, across a wide stretch of water, but even from a distance I could see her body language of complete puzzlement. She had turned expecting to see a blue boat with a woman driving only to find a man aboard a red boat entering the lock. She peered back down the canal baffled as to how 60 foot of steel had disappeared into thin air. Eventually she turned around and saw me glued to the opposite bank, grinning and waving. She trudged over to the other lock, glowered at me and went through all the palaver of opening that one as well. I told her it was good exercise. Opening heavy lock gates is as good as a work out at the gym but I don't know that that appeased her.

We negotiated the next two locks successfully with Jessica getting instructions from an upright, uptight character with a military moustache and a military bearing. He did everything, in a brisk and humourless fashion, by the book. It was a book I'd failed to find on the bookshelves. It was obvious he found us both sadly lacking in the essential skills and knowledge required for competent boating and wondered what on earth the world was coming to when people like us were allowed to roam freely on the waterways. I was surprised that Jessica didn't dump him in the canal, she doesn't usually suffer that sort of attitude kindly, but she smiled sweetly and did as she was told. Maybe the slow pace of canal life is therapeutic and it was having a calming effect on her.

We moored up for the day a few miles further along the canal and went off to experience the delights of the fleshpots of Rugby.

The next morning we set off early. I executed a perfect twenty eight point turn in a winding hole and we got back through the locks before the morning rush hour started. We moored at the other side of Hillmorton Locks to have a large breakfast (we felt we'd earned it) and then became trapped by an ever increasing traffic jam of boats waiting to go through the locks. There was a knock on the roof. I went out and the woman on the boat waiting alongside introduced herself as Rea's previous owner. I should have taken the opportunity to ask her what all the mysterious knobs and buttons are for and what was the funny noise when I switched on the gas and why she'd chosen to have red patterned curtains but I didn't I just mouthed pleasantries about what a lovely boat it was and she replied with pleasantries about how she hoped I'd enjoy owning her. Then the queue moved on and off she went. And to this day I still don't know what half the knobs and buttons are for and why there is still a funny noise when the gas is on. Although I do find this useful, if I forget to switch the hot water boiler off the annoying blip, blip, blip reminds me that it is still working away unnecessarily and eating gas.

Eventually we got out of the narrow boat jam and wended our way along the crowded canal. Reaching a long, straight, quieter stretch Jessica decided to have a try at steering. Two hundred yards further on we were entangled in an overhanging tree with ferocious, paint scraping, branches. It was all her fault of course. If she'd only looked at me instead of looking where she was going she would have seen my out-stretched left arm flapping madly and known she should take notice of the visual instruction to steer left and ignore the 'right, right, right!' that was spouting from my mouth.

After that the journey back was uneventful, we arrived home safely, albeit with a few more war wounds on the bow and paintwork.

The next day, once more securely moored in the marina, I took the empty wine bottles (did we really drink that much?) to the car, ready to take them to the bottle bank. I went to where I'd left the car and it wasn't there. I wondered if I'd put it somewhere else and stood still for a few minutes mentally retracing my steps of three days ago. Yes, I did leave it there. No, it wasn't there now. I later found out that it had been taken, driven across a field outside of Braunston and burnt out. Braunston: nice, neat, middle-class Braunston sitting prettily on its hill above the Grand Union canal is not the sort of place you expect this type of wanton vandalism to occur. I felt very let down by Braunston.

To look on the bright side one niggling concern had been eradicated. I had wondered how I would co-ordinate the moving of boat and car. How I would work out the logistics of move boat; find transport back to car; move car to boat; find somewhere to park car: move boat onwards; go back for car. Now that the car is a mere cinder in a Northamptonshire field I don't have to think about this.

No car. No problems. No worries.

The Start of The Journey

While I have been cleaning and polishing and having desultory conversations on the tow path, fifteen miles to the south the ex husband has finally bought a boat and is also trying to get used to living aboard.

He hasn't bought Melanie, the fresh blue and white boat he fell in love with, because as he predicted, somebody else had bought her before he had funds in place. He knew that would happen. He is not just a 'glass half empty' man, he is , 'glass half empty and it might as well have been completely empty because the contents will taste foul and most likely cause me an upset stomach,' man. My relentless optimism has always been a source of great irritation to him and probably was a contributory factor to the divorce.

I think he has bought a much better boat than the one he originally wanted. It's not as good as mine, of course, but it's a very masculine boat that has lots of dark wood panelling, impeccable paintwork and isn't lumbered with a silly, girlie name like Melanie.

I'd looked around for a winter mooring but it proved to be more difficult than I'd expected (note: all advice says find a mooring before buying a boat because there is a shortage of moorings, another bit of good advice that I ignored). My son points out that having two parents doing such a stupid thing as living on boats is a cause of concern to him and his sister. He feels the most sensible thing would be for us to travel together towards Cambridge and for both of us to stay around that area for the winter as we have friends and family who can keep an eye on us while we are learning about this new way of life. The ex already has a permanent site arranged and I eventually manage to find a winter mooring near Huntingdon so we will do as our son suggests and travel along together. For some reason the thought of us two travelling along the waterways side by side causes a great deal of amusement amongst my friends. I thought it would be fine, after all most of the time we would be at least sixty feet apart so there would be little opportunity for squabbles and harsh words. It should be all smooth sailing. I didn't envisage any problems.

I released the boat from the umbilical cord of the landline, negotiated successfully out of the marina and set off on a warm and sunny morning for the one and a half day journey to meet up with my Fellow Traveller. Feelings of trepidation alternated with feelings of excitement. With a little help I navigated the six locks from Braunston and set off to negotiate the Braunston tunnel. Unsurprisingly I am not looking forward to going through a long, dank, dark and claustrophobic tunnel.

When I enter the mouth of the mile long tunnel it feels like the beginning of a dark and dripping journey to the depths of the earth. Daylight disappears and the temperature drops to a clammy coolness. My headlight illuminates a low roof slimy with mould, stained with a century worth of grime. The lights inside the boat shine through the portholes and cause pale elliptical shapes to glide along the patched brickwork of the walls. The noise of the engine reverberates and the water churned by the propeller sploshes behind me. A faint patch of daylight from above is from the vent shafts that allow air in. I look up and the shafts are very grimy and very high, there must be an awful lot of hill above. The tunnel has a kink two thirds of the way along which means that the end is only faintly visible. One hundred years ago before the advent of directional technology two sets of workmen started digging at each end of the prospective tunnel and landslips meant they didn't quite meet in the middle, hence the kink.

Sod's law has it that the only other boat I meet is when I am approaching the kink. I stop and wait patiently until he passes me. Cold water drips down the back of my neck. Two narrow boats passing each other have about an inch to spare on either side yet we pass without contact. As he approaches I can only see the glare of his headlight, when his bow passes darkness descends again, the shape of his hull is dimly visible in the glow of my cabin lights and I can just discern a dark shape on the stern. I say brightly to the dark shape, 'It's a bit cold in here,' but the dark shape remains silent. Creepy. I feel as if I have been passed by a ghost boat. When I've safely negotiated the kink the light at the end of the tunnel glows but it still seems an age before I start to emerge into the outside world. On coming out of the gloom the bright sunshine and warm fresh air are delicious.

Then there is another flight of locks to negotiate but luckily I meet up with a hire boat with an excessive number of keen crew members so they do all the work and I go through the seven locks of the Buckby flight without having to make any effort whatsoever. I moor at Whilton for the night. On my left hand side is the M1, the roar of traffic is constant and when I wake up in the middle of the night I am under the impression that I have somehow managed to moor up on the hard shoulder of the motorway. On my right hand side is the mainline railway line to Birmingham; smart, sleek Virgin trains roar past at regular intervals. It shouldn't surprise me that the canal shares its route with roads and railways and rivers, it is logical that they would all use the same, easiest route around hills and through valleys. Just, somehow, I expected canals to make a lone, tranquil journey through unspoiled countryside far away from the noise of modern life but canals were built to service industry and run from city to city as do the roads and the railways.

The following morning I have a journey of twelve miles and no locks. It's a calm sunny day and I set off, negotiate a couple of narrow openings successfully and pass a couple of boats without hitting them. Suddenly I'm enjoying doing all this by myself; I'm honing my steering skills and at the same time waving to people on the towpath, making comments to boats passing by and smiling inanely at all and sundry. This is my boat and I am handling it by myself. I am proud and happy. The style of narrow boats on the Grand Union is varied. Free from the shackles of the marina I realise it's not just the Brians and Janets in their neat polished, flower be-decked boats who roam the canal system. There is the 'I wonder how that stays afloat?' boats of the live-aboards with a ton of wood, bikes, wheelbarrows and containers of herbs and vegetables on the roof. There are very short boats and very long boats and butties and tugs. There are boats that sell coal and wood and gas, a boat that announces that it is The Book Barge, another, The Cheese Boat, sells Welsh cheese. I try and think of the variety of Welsh cheeses it may sell; there's Caerphilly and umm Caerphilly and err…….. well there could be lots of cheeses made in Wales but Caerphilly is the only one I can think of.

Some of the boat names are interesting. I like Unthinkable but many that might have seemed a good idea after a few beers in the pub don't look so amusing in the cold light of day, Nice Butt…, Slowome, Mines a Pint. Dunworkin is the boating equivalent of the bungalow named Dunroamin. There appears to be a blazing row in progress onboard Tranquillity. I don't think I would have named my boat Wet Dream and there is a moored boat called My Fanny which surprises me, I wouldn't have thought anybody would want to sail around in a boat called My Fanny. Then I put my glasses on and see that it is called Myfanwy.

At lunchtime I arrive at where the prospective Fellow Traveller is waiting. He expects me to moor up behind him but I decide that it is too near a bend and there are two boats moored abreast across the canal and anyway that space doesn't look big enough for me to get into safely. I have grave doubts about my ability to slot the boat into, 'only just big enough' spaces. I carry on down the canal which displeases The Fellow

43

Traveller somewhat and he shouts a few words of advice after me, which, luckily, I can't hear over the noise of the engine. I progress slowly along the canal with the sound of his rancour gradually fading into the distance. I eventually find a space large enough for me to feel confident about getting into safely, namely a space large enough to take a freight train and a handful of articulated lorries. Ten minutes and one strained mobile telephone conversation later we decide he will join me and we'll have a quick lunch and set off. I don't bother expending too much energy hammering mooring pins into hard ground or tying the knots properly because I'm not staying long. I put the kettle on and stroll back along the towpath so I can indicate to him where Rea is waiting. I give him plenty of notice so he can slow down and moor up without having the extra stresses and strains of suddenly rounding the bend and having to stop and turn into a space quickly. He should be able to manage to moor up here easily after all there's still enough room behind me to park that freight train.

I can see him coming along the canal, I wave and point to my boat. He scowls and sticks a finger up. Obviously he hasn't yet forgiven me for not stopping where he decreed I should stop. I expect him to slow down but he doesn't, he wrestles with the tiller and comes into the bank at a sharp angle, even to my inexperienced eye his angles are wrong and his speed is excessive. He starts by smacking the boat that is moored the freight train length behind me. The boat that has been struck rocks violently, he turns and hurls curses at it, as if it had just leapt out at him unexpectedly and then he carries on still showing no sign of slowing down. He hits the bank which has also leapt out at him unexpectedly, bounces off it then heads straight towards Rea slamming into her stern. My lightly tapped in mooring pins go ping, ping, somersault into the air and splash into the canal. The momentum of the collision sends Rea away from the bank, and the pull of the wash from his boat drags her down the canal after him. So it would appear that we have started the journey: he is heading towards Gayton Junction, Rea is following behind as planned. The only flaw is I'm not standing at the tiller, I'm standing on the bank, open mouthed, wondering where my boat is going and how we are going to be reunited.

'Who was that bloody idiot?'

The man from the boat behind has come running, he looks as if he's been rudely awaken from an after lunch nap. He's tousled, bare-footed and blinking painfully in the bright daylight.

'No idea,' I say.

His boat has been hit hard, he's been abruptly woken up and he's after blood, he motors on down the bank shouting, then stands on something sharp, hops around a bit and hobbles back towards me. The blood he was after is disappearing into the distance so he re-directs his energy into working out how we get my boat back. We look at various options: get his boat hook and lean over and catch the trailing stern rope (too far away we might lean over and fall in), wait for another boat to come along to push us in (no boats in sight either way

45

down the canal) or get his boat to catch up with Rea and put me on board (it will take hours to untie and cast off and get me on board). By the time we've discussed the options the breeze has gently brought Rea back to the bank. My mooring pins have sunk, I can't moor up again easily so I decide to just get on board and carry on down the canal, lunchless, coffeeless and in a foul mood. Inside the cabin the kettle is whistling away merrily but the waiting mugs and their contents are strewn across the floor, along with the books that had been on the shelves and flowers and water that had been in a vase.

I eventually catch up with the useless prat that is to be my Fellow Traveller. He's lurking further down the canal well out of reach of angry boaters. I slow down and shout a few choice words, the most polite of which is, 'You owe me two mooring pin.' He's unrepentant, just says, 'Well.....' and scowls a lot, and replies to my abuse with a series of two finger exercises. So we navigate to Gayton Junction and I find two chains in place of the sunken pins and try and work out how to slot them into the armco and tie the ropes to them. We moor up in an aggressive silence and glare and stomp around, arrange our chains and ropes into a tangled mess and then retire to our respective boats for the night without a word passing between us. Wonderful, we're supposed to be travelling together for nearly two weeks and already, after only two hours on the same stretch of water, we've had a blazing row and we're not speaking to each other.

The following morning it's two dour and taciturn

novices planning to set sail. Single-handed, in tandem, not speaking or making eye-contact, leaving the canal system and travelling along the Nene to Peterborough, then across the Fens and onto the Great Ouse. I hope we are more competent than I feel, I hope we learn quickly how to handle these unwieldy lumps of metal, I hope he keeps well out of my way for the next two weeks.

The first day gets off to a bad start when trying to get off the bank and avoid moored boats we manage to crash into each other. Shortly afterwards we both crash into the same bridge, the smear of blue paint on the red brickwork is quickly over written by the smear of green. That's his impeccable paintwork gone to pot. He's peering over the side frowning at the scrapes, I'm smirking happily thinking this is just retribution for the loss of my mooring pins. Was it the warped sense of humour of Victorian engineers that meant every time they made a sharp bend they put a low brick bridge over it?

A mile down the canal we pick up our son who is going to act as an extra crew member to help us through the seventeen locks of the Northampton Arm and onto the River Nene. We decide we will take one boat through the first flight of thirteen locks and then go back for the other boat. My son and I build up a routine and take the Fellow Traveller's boat quickly and efficiently through the flight. Or maybe not quite as efficiently as I first imagined, as I'm going back up to collect my boat there are two walkers closing an open lock gate complaining about people who leave them open. I stop for a breather lean on the lock gate and join in the grumbling about inconsiderate people who don't close the gates behind them. Personally I blame hire boaters.

We get both boats through the first flight without too may bumps, bangs and cross words. We're now into September and darkness seems to fall early, at not much later than 7pm the day is drawing to an end. Although we are still on the canal system there has been a dearth of suitable places to moor. So we decide to tie up two abreast on a lock mooring at the entrance of one of the locks in the flight. In the eyes of Canal and River Trust and all rule book abiding boaters this is a most heinous crime. But we don't expect to be found out; we can see there isn't any traffic coming down the flight of locks behind us and as the light is failing we don't expect anyone to be coming up the canal.

The sun is a big red football balanced on the horizon, silhouetting a distant church tower. There is a mist settling over the fields where a flock of honking Canada Geese grazes. There is a cool smell of still water and freshly turned earth. Our moods have mellowed due to the successful negotiation of the series of locks, the calmness of the evening and the presence of a third party. The bottle of wine may also have helped.

We sit in the bow of the boat, resting, drinking wine and waiting for the chicken casserole to cook. The geese gradually cease their honking, the evening draws in gently and the only sound is the hum of traffic on the nearby but invisible M1. The waft of garlic and herbs from the oven is starting to smell tempting. Then in the distance we hear a faint chug, chug, chug and through the fading light and the rising mist a river cruiser materialises, slowly but determinedly approaching the lock.

We go forth to the lock to meet it, windlass in hand, helpful smiles pasted on, excuses ready for the, 'tut-tut-tut, you shouldn't be moored there,' head-shaking routine of the seasoned boater who knows all the rules.

We needn't have bothered formulating excuses for breaking the rules. It's three Brummie lads in a battered cruiser who don't know the rules and wouldn't give a stuff about them if they did.

'Know where the nearest pub is?' asks one as we wind up the paddles.

'There's none on the canal side. The nearest is after the next lock, it's about half an hour's walk across fields and down a lane.'

'Oh that's great, we love that, walking back over the fields by torchlight. Rob fell over a cow the other night. It's amazing, all that darkness and quietness and stars and stuff, you don't get proper dark in Birmingham.'

'Where have you travelled from?' I ask.

'Cambridge. We bought the boat in Cambridge. It's been a real adventure, started when we set off and turned left instead of right, went through the lock and then ended up amongst all these punts and rowing boats. We hadn't expected that. They was all shouting and yelling at us and then this official looking bloke comes alongside and tells us we'd turned the wrong way. Looked quite nice round there, all them old buildings but we didn't get a chance to look around much what with everybody getting mad and shouting. Then the next day we was in this great big lock and with one of those barge things you've got and another little boat like ours. When all the water gushed into the lock the big barge started banging about and sank the little bloke. We didn't hang about, as soon as that gate opened we were out of there, full throttle, wasn't going to give him the chance to sink us as well.'

He takes a drag on his cigarette and looks around. 'It's been an amazing week, all this countryside and some smashing pubs, a different one every night, even if we've had to walk miles to get to it. It's great when the full moon's out, all bright and silvery …. you never realise how bright moonlight is when you live in a city. Don't know how we're going to cope with living in Birmingham after seeing all this. Birmingham is going to be very dull.'

It's almost dark now and we stand by the canal watching the old river cruiser rise slowly in the filling lock. The cabin lights of the cruiser pick out the brickwork of the lock wall and reflect back onto the boat. It's a battle scarred old vessel, green mould around the windows, a crack on the deck, bits of trim missing, paintwork peeling.

Its owner stands back and looks at it proudly. I look at it and wonder why he went all the way to Cambridge to buy an old wreck, surely there were old wrecks for sale nearer to home. He must have read my thoughts. 'It was new when we got it.' he said.

On Wider Waters

The first two miles of the Northampton Arm passes through the same gentle West Northamptonshire countryside that has surrounded me since I left Braunston. The last two miles drop down into the outskirts of Northampton. The reeds and weeds at the side of the canal cause it to become narrow and it is strewn with rubbish. I manage to avoid a submerged bicycle but something hard, nasty and hidden from view clanks on the bottom of the boat and the propeller becomes fouled by a plastic bag and quantities of weed. I've been shown how to remove foreign bodies from the propeller. It looks easy: lift the back bit that I stand on (it probably has a proper name but I haven't learned the proper names yet), unscrew the hatch that guards the box over the propeller, lift hatch cover, remove all the bits of junk from the prop, put cover back in place, screw back on tightly. The last bit is essential because if the weed hatch cover is badly fitting or loose the water comes in and the boat sinks. I don't want that to happen after only three weeks of boat ownership. Of course I was shown how to do it by a man with muscles and long arms who had spent a life-time grovelling around in weed hatches. Lifting the back bit that I stand on was easy but it all went downhill from there. I couldn't undo the screw handle that held the weed hatch on and had to get the mallet to whack it open. The cover was heavy and low in the bowels of the boat and I had visions of dropping it into the irretrievable depths of the stern. The water was so murky that I couldn't see what was fouling the prop and even when I lay flat on my stomach (as flat as my far from flat stomach would allow) my arms weren't long enough to reach the tangle of obstruction. So then it was a case of poking it with bits of wood, a screwdriver and the bread knife to loosen the rubbish and remove it. Then I had to strain my back and feeble biceps to lift the cover back in place, hammer it tight, and cross my fingers that I had done it all correctly and wasn't going to travel along oblivious to the water gushing into the bilges and sinking the boat.

The last two locks on the Northampton Arm, which are padlocked to prevent vandalism, are adorned with red and black graffiti. On the bars of the last two lock gates the graffiti states, 'Nathan Bugg is a grass and is gay.' Another hand adds, 'So is his father' and as an afterthought scrawls underneath, 'and his brother'. More literature on the lock casts further aspersions on the loyalty, sexuality and parentage of Nathan Bugg and his family.

As we come to the last lock on our way to the Nene a narrow boat is heading back towards the canals. The couple on board tell me they had planned to go down the Nene but once they'd turned off the canal onto the river the wideness and mass of water had scared them so they'd turned round and were going straight back onto the canal system.

When I steer my boat out of the canal and onto the river I see what they mean. The canals do encourage a form of agoraphobia their shallowness and narrowness make the boater feel snug and safe. The river is wide and the water is deep and, unlike the water on the canals, it moves. There has been quite a lot of overnight rain recently and there is a noticeable flow on the river. I suddenly feel as if I have been thrown out into a big, bad world and I'm being daring and brave: an intrepid explorer. You could say I'm having an adventure. Yet I also feel liberated. This is better. I am now on proper living water, not the murky stagnant stuff that masquerades as water on the canal system. I'm a proper boater now.

We moor up at the Town Quay in Northampton to release our crew member back into civilization. He heads to the bus station like a scalded cat, no doubt happy to be away from the warring factions on the two boats. We're going to the supermarket to re-stock the fridges and then carry on up the Nene.

I wait patiently for the Fellow Traveller to finish faffing with his ropes so we can walk into the town. It will probably take him a long time. If faffing ever becomes an Olympic sport he would be a gold medal contender. To pass the time I read the sign on the footbridge that crosses the river. It's called The Wathen Wigg Bridge, named as the result of a competition. It commemorates the Reverend Samuel Wathen Wigg who started a rugby club for boys called the Northampton St James which became Northampton Rugby Club (which explains why they are known as The Saints). I wonder what other suggestions they got for the name of the bridge. I bet there were some more

53

interesting and some more unprintable ones. All others must have been easier to pronounce than The Wathen Wigg Bridge. Try repeating it quickly: The Wathen Wigg Bridge. The Wathen Wigg Bwidge. The Waffen Widge Bwidge. At closing time in Northampton on a Saturday night it could be a test of sobriety, if you can walk in a straight line and say The Wathen Wigg Bridge, perfectly, six times then you are fit to drive home in the motor vehicle of your choice.

The bridge is painted in Northampton Rugby Club's colours, which are obviously green and yellow with smears of black mould. Green and yellow may be suitable colours for rugby shirts but they don't do a lot for bridges. I decide the bridge would look better if it was painted black. A black bridge would be much more tasteful. I wonder if Northampton Rugby Club could be persuaded to change their team colours to black to match the bridge. Then they could be called The All Blacks instead of The Saints. I bet nobody's thought of that name before.

The Fellow Traveller still hasn't joined me and my attention has shifted from suitable colour schemes for bridges to calculating the percentages of blinds to curtains at the windows of the flats lining the quay when an elderly man in mangy grey trousers, sporting an ineffective comb-over and leaning on crutches, hobbles up.

'You're back then.' he says.

'Yes.' I say.

'You remember I was at B&Q the last time you were here?'

54

'Yes.' I say.

'Well I've moved now, I'm at the new moorings near the town. I've left B&Q because the boat got broken in to. They nicked my 32 inch TV and all my camera equipment. I got robbed twice, once by the gits that broke in and the second time by the thieving insurance company. The bloody insurance companies are the worst thieves of the lot. Then to make matters worse my legs went bad. Marion's been helping me. You remember Marion?'

'Errmmm…'

'She's beautiful is Marion, only forty two and wonderful to me. I got a bit down about everything. I said I'm going to end up in a wheelchair in a care home and Marion said you may be in a wheelchair but I'll never let you go into a care home, you'll always have a home with me. I'm a lucky man, she's only forty two and beautiful. Phorrr she's beautiful.'

With that he turned and shambled away, muttering, 'Phorr she's beautiful,' at frequent intervals as he hobbled off down the quayside. I watched his retreating back, puzzled. As far as I can remember I've never been to downtown Northampton in my life.

Who was he? Do I know Marion? What's B&Q got to do with it? How did he fit a 32 inch television on a boat? Who does he think I am?

I assume he recognised the boat. Rea has had one careful lady owner (and if she thinks she's got another lady owner that's careful then she's in for a shock). When I was travelling along the Grand Union standing at the tiller I have seen people waving enthusiastically

55

at me; as I draw near the waving arm starts to flag and then fades away completely and the hand is stuffed firmly in a pocket as if to stem its wayward, flamboyant behaviour. When I pass they realise I am not who they expected me to be and I have to make do with a slightly sheepish smile and a brief nod.

Eventually, after The Fellow Traveller's ropes are arranged into a design that would win any international macramé competition, we set off to do the shopping. I will not be taking full advantage of this rather useful forty eight hour mooring to explore Northampton as this is only a brief, fridge re-stocking stop. I'm sure if I'd approached Northampton by road once I'd passed the ninety eight roundabouts, the out of town Tesco's, Halfords and Carpets R Us, I'd have been told that it is an historic market town and there would have been lots of brown signs pointing out places of interest to visit. I'm sure that there will be a lumpy mound where there used to be a castle and an historic market square. I'm certain that somewhere or other there will be a shoe museum for Northampton was famous for the manufacture of shoes. But for my first visit to Northampton a trip to Morrisons will have to suffice. Wide rivers, yellow bridges, sexually charged old men and busy supermarkets. There is only so much excitement a woman can cope with in one day.

Fridge fully stocked I untie and head for the first lock on the Nene. Having taken an age to tie his ropes securely the Fellow Traveller now takes an age to untie them. He then discovers the first major difference between the river and the canal. Rivers have currents.

He unties the stern first, then the centre rope and then heads towards the bow rope. Even on a calm day on the still waters of the canals this is not the most sensible order for a single handed boater to use to untie the ropes. On a river with a strong flow of water it's asking for trouble. His complex system of knots is designed to stop anybody easily setting the boat free. It not only stops passing thieves, vandals and groups of lads who think it's good fun to watch a boat floating off downriver it also stops its owner, especially when that owner is starting to panic. As the boat moves the knots tighten and the task of unravelling them becomes even more difficult. Looking behind me I can see his state of desperation setting in. I moor up at the lock and start to go back to help but a young man has stepped in and between them they manage to untie the boat. The boat has now turned one hundred and eighty degrees and is facing in the opposite direction, the centre rope trailing in the river.

The young man holds the bow rope until The Fellow Traveller retrieves his centre rope and gets back on the tiller. Then he has to turn the boat around to face in the right direction. I decide to offer some helpful advice, along the lines of, 'Let the current take the bow,' and, 'Go forward gently'. He can't hear me because he now has the engine in full throttle and his brain in full panic. I shout louder to make myself heard over the engine, I might as well have saved my breath to cool my porridge as my Grannie used to say. I should know that the last thing anybody can hear with an engine roaring in their ears is a stream of useless instructions shouted from the riverbank. Hearing the shouting a small group of spectators start to gather. The Fellow Traveller can't hear what I'm saying but he can see my mouth moving so assumes I'm shouting abuse. He shouts a few instructions back at me.

'Oh, that wasn't a very nice thing to say,' remarks a woman standing beside me, 'especially when you were only trying to be helpful.'

I turn my back on him and go ahead and put my boat into the lock and wait patiently for him to join me. And Wait. And Wait. Eventually he comes in alongside me giving my stern a solid thump as he drives into the narrow space. We stand side by side at our tillers, staring ahead in stony silence. Our truce as we came up the Northampton Arm was brief.

The boater waiting to come upriver operates the lock for us but leaves one of the top lock paddles open and when the bottom lock is opened to let the water out the turbulence this causes sends my tiller swinging wildly and implants two large bruises on my spare tyre. I've always taken Martin's advice and stood in the well of the boat, had I been on the back the force of the swinging tiller could have pushed me into the water. I wonder if something similar had happened to a woman who, only a few weeks previously, had fallen from a narrow boat into a lock and had died.

So if Martin's advice has saved me from serious injury or even death then his lesson was worth the time and money despite all the things I may have been saying to the contrary.

The Queen of The Nene

Two locks further down from the Becketts Park Lock the Nene is flooding over the top of the upstream gate and we can't get the downstream lock to equalise and open. After an hour of struggling we give in and ring the Environment Agency number which is on the sign on the bankside and ask for advice and they say they will send someone out to help. We take the boats out of the lock (not sure why we did that) and tie up at the lock mooring and wait for the Environment Agency man to come over from Oundle.

While we are waiting a narrow boat arrives, with the mandatory Brian and Janet on board. They go straight into the lock and we explain the difficulties we've been having. This is a couple unfazed by an uncooperative lock, they are experienced boaters, not nervous novices like us. They have seen it all before, they have been up and down the Nene for years, they know every lock and its idiosyncrasies, they know every bend, every boater, every reed and every duck. She knows Roy the man we're waiting for ('He'll blame me, he blames me for everything that happens on the river'). They know how to deal with this lock. She skips from boat to bank with a nimbleness that belies her age and quickly and efficiently operates the lock. He ties a rope around the forward lock gate. When the water seems to equalise the three of us heave on the lock gates and he reverses the boat pulling on the ropes. The gates gradually wheeze open enough for the boat to drive through, she leaps back on board unfastens the ropes, and sits cross-legged on the bow, a grey-haired figurehead on an elderly blue boat, the Queen of the Nene. Then they glide off into the early evening, with neither a wave nor a backward glance.

We feel a bit silly when Roy turns up. If the other boat could manage it shouldn't we be able to? But he is friendly and helpful and doesn't treat us like idiots. He says there are often problems with this lock, thinks it may be something jammed in the paddle. I ask the inane question 'Do you think it might be a body?' so we have a few minutes' conversation about bodies in locks as he refills it. Then he opens it effortlessly.

It is getting late when we get going again and the light is starting to fade. My map tells me there are moorings about half an hour ahead at Weston Favell but when we get there they appear to be full. I'm the lead boat so go around the sharp bend under the bridge hoping that there are more moorings. Immediately after the bend there is only the lock and it already has two boats in it heading upstream towards us. I'm mooring up on the lock landing when the Fellow Traveller comes ricocheting around the bend thumping into the bridge and then finds he has nowhere to go because if he moored alongside me he would block the exit from the lock. He yells abuse at me for leading him down a blind alley. When the boats come out of the lock he goes in, and we have a discussion (well it's a bloody great row actually) about what we're going to do. It's getting dark so we decide to spend another night illegally parked on a lock mooring. He'll go through and moor on the downstream lock platform. I'll stay where I am. It's best if there's at least a seventy foot lock between us because we're on the point of mutual murder (not for the first time in our long history) and the further apart we are the better it will be. We decide to move off early the next day before anybody comes along telling us we shouldn't be here.

The mechanism of this lock is different from any I've come across before. It has a guillotine gate with keys and knobs and buttons so I'm peering at the operating instructions in the fading light when the Queen of the Nene and her dog materialise on the opposite bank. I think she's come to help us but she hasn't, she is simply here to point out our deficiencies.

'What do you think you are doing? she yells across the lock.

'Learning to tap-dance,' I mutter.

I prod a button and the lock gate starts to clank upwards, obliterating most of her words.

'You can't stay here .... clank, grind, clunk....there was plenty of room back there you should have moored alongside .... grind, grind, clank ..... against the rules, don't you know about.....grind, grind, clank.... selfish people like you that ruin it for the rest of decent boa .... clank, clunk, grind ..... wasting water, you should have two boats ....grind, grind, grind ... can't handle the boats properly shouldn't be on the river .... clank, clunk, THUD.'

I untie the Fellow Traveller's boat and throw the rope down to him, hoping to hit him between the eyes but my aim is as bad as ever and it lands limply on the roof. He moves his boat out of the lock and I'm left standing opposite the Queen of the Nene and she's still in full flow.

'We'd saved you a space but ...'

'Sod off.' I shout 'It's been a long day, I don't need to listen to you, so just SOD OFF!'

She looks amazed, stands open-mouthed for a few seconds and then turns on her heels and sods off. Her black dog hesitates for a few more seconds then sods off after her.

I cross the footbridge to get back to my boat and some horses in the adjoining field wander over. They're the black and white chunky, hairy, variety of horse with big feet and feathered hocks. One leans towards me, I give him a scratch between the ears, he wickers gently and I stay to stroke his nose. It's soft and pink and velvety, and as I stroke him I start to relax and my frazzled nerves begin to repair. He moves nearer. I rub his neck gently. He bites me hard, leaving a red welt on my forearm.

Northamptonshire

We left Weston Favell early the next morning before anybody else appeared and harangued us for breaking all the rules of boating. We ploughed on leaving the conurbation of Northampton behind, passing the chalets of Billing Aquadrome and the marina which lurks behind them. We moored against an extensive, cow studded, water meadow at Coggenhoe for a late breakfast and half an hour after we'd stopped who should come chugging down the river but the Queen of the Nene and her consort.

I tell The Fellow Traveller, 'Ignore them. She's going to tell us we shouldn't be here and we've hammered our pins in illegally and we're a hazard to all passing boats. Whatever the old bitch says just ignore them.'

They draw level with my boat, where we're sitting in the bow drinking unexpectedly harmonious mugs of coffee. The Queen of the Nene is standing in the bow of their boat with the dog by her side and both are staring resolutely into the far distance. The consort slows down. 'If you'd like to travel along with us we'll help you through the locks,' he says. His smile is friendly and he's trying to be helpful. I wonder if she went back last night and reported what I'd said. It's likely they've had a long life together and many a time he's wanted to tell her to 'Sod Off' so he's feeling particularly warm towards somebody who has done so.

I smile frostily and say, 'We're stopping here for a while and thank you for the offer but we don't need any help.' The Fellow Traveller takes absolutely no notice of my instructions to ignore them, gets off the boat and strolls alongside as they move towards the lock, chatting happily to them. Once I am out of eye contact range the Queen of the Nene stops looking into the far distance and joins in the conversation. It could be The Fellow Traveller is a kind and forgiving person but it is more likely that he prefers to be on the side of the team that upset me. I stay where I am. I'm not a kind and forgiving person. I can bear a grudge for years over the smallest of slights, I can bear a grudge long after I have forgotten why I'm bearing a grudge. After a few hours, two locks and five miles of river I most certainly haven't forgotten why I'm bearing a grudge nor have I forgiven her, there's still enough of my grudge left to last until the end of her days.

After they'd gone through the lock and we had given them time to get well ahead we moved off. We passed the flooded disused gravel pits and through the mixture of scrubby landscape and quiet countryside. At Wollaston Lock a farmer leaning on a fence surrounded by a flock of yellow eyed, bored looking sheep advises us not to stop or even slow down in Wellingborough and to make sure all the doors are closed when we speed through. 'Wellingborough is full of toe-rags who jump on boats and nick anything that isn't nailed down,' he tells us, 'Get through Wellingborough as fast as you can.' We ignore his good advice and moor overnight in Wellingborough.

Like Northampton might well have been, Wellingborough might also be a town awash with places of fascinating historical interest. I didn't bother going to look for these, I just pop into the nearby Tesco to buy some more strong alcohol. I seem to be in need a lot of strong alcohol on this trip. There was one other boat moored on the embankment where we stopped, a couple who had come out for a weekend jaunt. They had a permanent mooring at Willy Watts Marina at Ringstead, about ten miles downstream. They'd set chairs on the bankside and were sitting happily by the boat on the edge of a park amidst overflowing litter bins and dog deposits listening to the roar of traffic on the bypass and gazing at the high blank walls of Whitworths' factory. Ringstead is in a pretty area and if you are going to spend a mild September evening sitting by a riverbank with a bottle of wine it would seem a much more pleasant place to do so than the middle of Wellingborough. The old adage, 'A change is as good as a rest,' came to mind and I suppose scenery can become rather tedious and a factory wall and a rubbish strewn river does at least make a bit of a change.

After a peaceful and trouble free night in Wellingborough we carried on and stopped for a lunch in Irthlingborough. A passing dog walker stopped to chat and told me that the classic 1910 film Waterloo was made here. 'If it hadn't been for the First World War Irthlingborough would have been the centre of the film industry, not Hollywood.' He may be right but I looked around and found it difficult to imagine Clark

Gable lounging on a sunbed at the side of the in-filled gravel pits or Humphrey Bogart and Lauren Bacall strolling along Irthlingborough High Street in the drizzle.

Parts of Northamptonshire are pleasant enough but I can't think it is likely that the English equivalent of Beverley Hills would have sprung up amongst its gentle contours. Although for centuries Northamptonshire has been known as the county of Squires and Spires so it must have a reputation for having some well-heeled inhabitants.

In Northampton and Wellingborough the spires were hidden amongst the breweries, warehouses and high rise flats. There weren't any sightings of potential squires in either town and I can't think that squires are thick on the ground in Daventry, Corby and Kettering either. Or maybe it was just that they had discarded the traditional squire garb of tweeds and brogues and had donned jeans and anoraks to merge with the locals standing in the bus queues. Or maybe in Wellingborough, in the town park where we'd moored the previous night, the squires were hidden under hoodies so they could make furtive purchases from the back of the black van that was parked in a dark corner. If the resident squires have tried to disguise their appearance they have done so effectively.

When we left Irthlingborough our surroundings began to change. In Wellingborough the dogs being walked along the banks of the Nene were a ferocious looking lot. They were short haired, blunt faced, barrel chested and bow legged. They strained at the leash and snarled at the other dogs. The theory that dog-owners look like their dogs held true for the locals around here. They were shaven headed, barrel chested, had short legs and shouted at their dogs and snarled at passers-by. The only discernible difference was the number of tattoos the owners sported. In general the dogs seemed to be tattoo free.

A few miles further on the appearance of the dogs and the dog walkers along the Nene Way changed. Status dogs are replaced by lifestyle dogs. Here both the dogs and their owners have a traceable family lineage, are vitamin enriched, sport shiny tresses and boundless energy. They'd both look good stretched out in front of the Aga waiting for Country Life to come around for the photo shoot.

As we are going through Ringstead Lock an elderly man wanders over from Willy Watts Marina to greet Rea's owner then finds out the owner isn't who he thought it was and gets cross with me for being somebody else. After I've apologised for being me and not being somebody else he does give us some useful information: the moorings at Woodford which are shown on our map and where we are heading no longer exist so once again we break the rules and moor up on the lock landings. The day is gradually going to bed, discarding the harsh light of afternoon and donning the mellower, softer, mistier shades of evening. The wind drops and the river flattens and becomes a smooth sheet broken only by the fish jumping and leaving ever increasing circles on the viscous, darkening surface. Swallows dart across the surface of the water catching insects, packing in as much food as possible before their imminent departure to Africa.

I am mesmerised by the reflections of trees and clouds in the water. The definition of the trees is stronger on the surface of the water than the originals on the bank. The reflected colours of the pink tinged clouds are more intense than the pink tinged clouds that float above us. The slight shimmer of the water gives a new life and fresh dimensions to the reflections. As it becomes darker I can no longer see the fence which lines the bank yet its reflection on the still river remains bright, clear and well defined.

As the moon rises its reflection takes over from the fading reflections of the trees and clouds. A silver globe rests on the surface and its silver light spreads across the river.

We decide to walk the mile up the road to the pub and take a torch to light the way. For a pair of townies who are used to well-lit streets walking in the darkness of the countryside, lit only by the light of the moon and the feeble beam of a cheap torch, feels quite an adventure. My eyes take a while to adjust to the light and are then rapidly unadjusted by the glaring headlights of oncoming traffic.

On this Monday evening the pub is quiet, it's just us and a team practising for a pub skittles contest. I haven't seen a game of skittles quite like this. It's on a table rather than a skittle alley. I'm told it's unique to Northamptonshire and the pub league is competitive.

We don't stay long, we just have a couple of drinks and leave. On the way back to the boats, stumbling through the darkness, we can see an orange glow from a town and on a distant parallel road white headlights sweep across black spaces. Something scuffles in the hedgerows, an owl calls in the distance and overlaying all the rustles and squeaks and squawks is the hum of traffic on a distant road. Is there anywhere in England where the hum of traffic is totally absent?

Northamptonshire is Nice

After Ringstead the Nene becomes a meandering, quintessentially English river, winding its way gently through fields and woods and reed beds and banks. Curious calves, supping at the river, lift their heads and watch us glide past, scenic sheep graze on verdant meadowland. Reeds, pink willowherb and purple loosestrife stirred in the breeze, willows dip into the water and the silvered leaves of the alders whispered in the breeze. Geese, ducks and swans float by, a grebe fed her youngster with a silvery fish that looks too big to go down its scrawny throat. A posse of white, yellow beaked ducks, escapees from a child's picture book, filed out of the river and trooped up the bank. Herons stand immobile by the riverside then, suddenly aware of the presence of the boat, they take flight tucking in their chins as they slowly and elegantly flap across the river, their legs trailing and then being gradually laid against their bodies. The gentle hills slope up to villages hidden amongst stands of trees and a plethora of spires punctuated the horizon.

This is the type of countryside where one would expect squires to lurk. I relax and imagine one, he's cantering his dock tailed cob across these smooth green fields. He's a tweed coated, leather gaitered and bareheaded squire. I am with him as he passes through the white painted gate to the honey stoned manor house, coming home in time for an afternoon tea served on a flowered, porcelain tea service. I imagine him clattering into an immaculate, cobbled stable yard and handing his horse to a groom. My imaginings are at least a century out of date but all the more pleasant because of that. Then I am brought back to the reality of now when the boat ploughs into the bank.

The problem with the meandering, quintessentially English rivers is that they demand total concentration if all the bends are to be negotiated successfully.

The writer H.E. Bates was born in this region of Northampton at nearby Rushden. While his famous books about the Larkin family, which were made into the TV series The Darling Buds of May, were set in the more bucolic countryside of the Kent hop fields many of his earlier stories and novels, including Love for Lydia, were inspired by this rural landscape where he grew up. Viewed from the middle of the river this landscape would appear to have changed little since he wrote his books and short stories.

Northamptonshire is also called The Forgotten County. It is the part of the country that people pass through on their way from North to South or East to West but don't think of as a destination. In the west of the county the buildings are built of the local Marlstone stone which is an unappetising dark brown. To the east the local stone of which the older houses are built is a paler, much more attractive, creamy colour. This mellow colour of the houses and villages and the sheep grazing amongst the hills make it seem a scaled down version of the Cotswolds, a version of the Cotswolds without the steepness of the hills and the smugness of the inhabitants. Instead of The County of Squires and Spires or The Forgotten County I think they could use the slogan 'Northamptonshire is Nice'. I admit it does lack the zing that a dynamic, forward thinking county would wish for as a slogan and a branding agency wouldn't recommend it but I think it is an apt description for this part of Northamptonshire. It is very nice.

Onwards on The Nene

The next morning it's up early and on our way again. The sun is out and it's warm and still. The Gods must be smiling on us to provide such perfect weather for our journey. By this stage the Fellow Traveller and I have got a system for going through the locks. We moor up, close the guillotine gates and fill the lock. Then we both open the upriver gates, drive in and close them behind us. Then he ties the boats together and stays on the tiller using the throttle to keep them both steady. I go and let the water out and then open the guillotine gates. This isn't usually an onerous task because most of them are mechanized. When they aren't mechanised (because there is no power to an isolated lock) there is a large wheel to turn manually and then closing and opening the gate is very hard work. I feel then that the balance of labour is unfairly weighted in my direction. Once the gate has been re-opened I climb down the ladder and step onto the front of the boat, walk through the boat, emerge at the back and then we untie the boats and carry on downriver. The only marginally tricky bit is climbing down the greasy, wet, weed strewn ladder into a deep lock and stepping onto the gunwales trying not to get entangled with the cratch cover (that damn thing has got to go). Mostly it works satisfactorily and I don't slip and fall in. Of course, there are a few spats and a few sharp words are exchanged but mostly the routine runs almost smoothly.

By the time we reached Woodford Lock the Fellow Traveller was irritating me. I'm not sure what he was doing to irritate me, probably breathing. I do my tasks and climb down the ladder. It's a slimy ladder and I don't find it easy to get my footing and he doesn't seem to be able to get the boats lined up with the ladder which only increases my irritation. Eventually I take a leap of faith, land on the gunwale and scramble into the boat. Being spiteful I don't tell him I'm going for a pee and that I'm putting the kettle on ready to make a cup of coffee. For good measure I check my phone for messages and then wander slowly to the back of the boat. The time lapse between seeing me climb down the ladder and arrive out the back has obviously seemed endless to him. He has imagined the worst, out of his sight I must have had a dreadful accident; if I'd fallen in he wouldn't have heard the splash over the sound of the engines so he has worked himself into a complete tizz.

'What happened?' he yells.

'Didn't you hear me shout I was going to the lavatory?' I say, trying my best to adopt an expression of puzzled innocence.

'No, I thought you'd fallen in. I was getting frantic.'

I look at his face, it's creased with worry. The stress of the last few minutes is clearly visible. I lean over to untie the ropes, smirking to myself. Serves him right for saying whatever it was he said to upset me.

At Thrapston the busy A14 crosses the river and I am reminded that I am only about twenty miles away from my ultimate destination, the marina at Buckden. Half an hour by road, a week by water, I could walk it in a fraction of the time it will take on this slow boat on this meandering river and then long loop around the Fens and onto the great Ouse. I suddenly have a great, aching longing to be in amongst the traffic on that busy road, getting there quickly instead of floating along at four miles an hour amidst idyllic scenery. Their journeys seem busy and purposeful; my life seems purposeless and empty. I feel I'm just drifting. Many times I've driven along the A14, looked at the river and wished I was calmly floating along it, never thinking I would change the role of harassed driver to the role of laid back boater. Now I am on the water wishing I could change once more to the role of harassed driver. There's just no pleasing some people.

I'm still not relaxed in my role as a single-handed boater. I still wake up in the morning and worry about the day ahead and how I'm going to cope with the driving (or helming or sailing, whatever the right term may be) and hope I don't do anything stupid or dangerous. Once I'm standing at the tiller of the boat the sun dissipates my worries as effectively as it dissipates the morning mist on the river. I feel confident and in control and the only times (well many times, actually) I do lose control and plough into the bank is when I'm gazing around and enjoying the countryside or watching the wildlife instead of looking where I'm going. Each lock mooring, each overnight mooring, I manage to get onto neatly, I don't crash into anybody or cause any damage to property or other boats or to myself. Yet in the early hours of the morning I wake up worrying. I have strange dreams about crashing boats and driving over weirs and the next morning when it is time to get up I have a knot of worry in my stomach and have serious doubts about my ability to handle the boat safely. Maybe I'm not suited to this kind of life, maybe I should pack it in now and go and live in a house and get a job and buy a very, very fast car.

I leave the A14 behind, manoeuvre through the correct arch of the ancient nine arched bridge at Thrapston without taking any of it with me and move on uneventfully. Coming into Titchmarsh the church I can see on my left at Aldwincle is probably the one where John Dryden, playwright, poet and the first Royal Poet Laureate was born in 1631. He was born in the rectory when his grandfather was the rector of All Saints church. The imposing church is now redundant and empty. The old rectory opposite is now called Dryden House and that's about the only mention of the village's famous son.

Reaching Wadenhoe we moor at the end of the garden of The Kings Head. It's early afternoon, warm sunshine glows on the honeyed stone houses. Wadenhoe is a very attractive village: a pub on the top of the hill, a narrow street flanked by thatched cottages and renovated barns, a manor house, a converted mill by the old mill pond. Chaffinch peck for insects in the lichen covered stone walls, two alpaca (an animal that must have been designed by a toy manufacturer) gaze over the fence. A red kite floats overhead. The mellowness of the scene amidst the soft warmth of the autumn afternoon permeates our mood as we take the path up the hill towards the small mostly 13th Century church of St Michael and All Angels with its distinctive squat tower. We then head upwards through fields of sheep to the Lyveden Way which continues to Lyveden New Bield.

I find the name Lyveden New Bield odd. Surely it should be 'New Build' but evidently 'bield' is a word for a symbolic lodge. The symbolic lodge at Lyveden was started but never finished. It sits remotely on the top of a hill surrounded by open grasslands, which were to be a deer park. There is a moat. The walls of the lodge are solid and the rooms complete but the building is roofless and windows gaze, emptily across open countryside. The interior has never had the floors installed and the only interior embellishments are Catholic statuary. Yet its solidity and position give it a huge presence. There were plans for extensive gardens. The work was started in 1595 and ten years later stopped on the death of Sir Thomas Tresham who had commissioned the project. As the Catholic family was later implicated in the gunpowder plot they rather fell out of favour with the rulers of the country and all work on the house and garden was abandoned. During the Second World War the Luftwaffe took aerial photographs of the area and the original layout of the gardens, labyrinth and orchards were revealed. The National Trust has the original plans and correspondence between Sir Thomas and his gardener. They have planted trees in the orchard using the species of apple, plums and pears that were originally used.

77

The grass is cut so that the outline of the labyrinth is clearly visible.

As the sun is getting low in the sky and there is a faint haze lying across the grass and fields this is a wonderfully quiet and calm place to be, or at least it would be if The Fellow Traveller would stop talking. I wander away from him trailing my hand on the warm rough stone. The lower walls are covered in graffiti, not the lurid spray painted graffiti of the urban tags that litter buildings and roadsides, this is carefully chiselled graffiti dating back three centuries but all the same it is still graffiti.

In 1747 J Guess chiselled his name, in 1881 it was J M Dewsbury, in 1883 it was J Pulpher, in 1990 it was Bob Willis and Ange. The walls of Lyveden New Bield are covered with the scratchings and scrapings of centuries. In many cases the lettering has become almost illegible and only the faint impressions remain. Who were these people who came to this remote building armed with implements to engrave their names in the soft stone? They were a formal bunch these long gone vandals, they signed their initials and surname, usually in copy book engraving. S. Snaith 1796 was deeply etched. William Goldman, a rare use of a forename, etched his so perfectly that one imagines his day job was that of a stonemason. Trev didn't put the date against his name but I suspect he was a more recent addition, as is Punks. The handwriting gives it away it is scrawled and scruffy. The computer age has ruined the etchings of the youth of this country, back in the eighteenth century the youth had chiselling to be

78

proud of.

As the sun started to set we went back down the hill in a companionable silence and on to the pub; it was only fair we were using their moorings. In the pub a team where practising skittles in preparation for a match in the Northamptonshire pub league.

Recalcitrant Rope

I may have gone to bed in a state of cider induced mellowness but the next morning I still wake up with a knot of worry in my stomach. I decide I want a day off. We were moored in a lovely place at the end of the garden of a friendly pub serving good food. The sun is shining and a blustery wind is scudding a few fluffy clouds across the dark blue of the sky. There are a myriad of footpaths through attractive countryside, countryside that I may never visit again. It seemed a pity to go charging down a river (if travelling at four miles an hour can be considered to be charging) and never giving ourselves time to explore the area beyond the bank. I had a good internet connection on my dongle, I need to catch up on work and emails, I need to wash some knickers, I needed to check things on the boat (not sure what or how but I'm sure I could find something to fiddle with), I need to do all the things I had been too tired to do at the end of the travelling day. The things that I need to do, the reasons I could list for staying put for a day were endless even if the real reason was that I was just want a break from standing on the back of a boat for eight hours each day.

The Fellow Traveller didn't agree with me. We should, 'Push On!' His reasons for pushing on were as endless as mine were for staying put, the main one being that if he didn't get to Ely within a week he might lose his chance of a permanent, residential mooring and if that should happen it would be, 'My Fault!' I reluctantly agreed and cheered myself with the notion that, 'Pushing On!' would shorten the time I had to spend in his company. I forcefully pointed out that I had been travelling two more days than he had and I was tired and people make mistakes when they are tired and if I made mistakes it was, 'His Fault!'

I am a great believer in the power of positive thinking and today it worked. I was positive things would go wrong so they did.

It hadn't been me that nearly drove over the weir, it hadn't been me that left the keys in the lock mechanism and had to walk back two miles to retrieve them, it hadn't been me that had problems mooring, or who nearly demolished a lock gate. It hadn't been me that constantly got the centre rope tangled in all the cack on the roof of the boat. I thought I was handling this boating lark much more competently than the Fellow Traveller because I calculated I was making fewer mistakes. I was feeling smug and superior and I was making sure the smugness and superiority were known to the other party.

Then along came the wind and all my gentle, gliding techniques that had worked well on the calm days we had encountered so far were useless when a gale was blowing across the fields accompanied by a strong draw from sluices and weirs. The Fellow Traveller's more gung-ho boating technique meant he handled these changed conditions much better than I did.

We had to leave the mooring in the by-way at Wadenhoe by reversing out. He reversed out faultlessly, moored by the lock and waited for me. Over the next half hour he had occasional glimpses of the stern of my boat, he could hear the revving of engines, smell overheated diesel and listen to a constant stream of bad language because every time I nearly got out the wind blew me back in. He could only wait patient and puzzled until I eventually joined him. Then I left the keys in the lock mechanism and he had to go back for them (I decided he was nearer).

An hour or so later than anticipated we were on our way again. The day was blustery but sunny. White clouds scurried and a group of red kites floated on the wind. Watching ten red kites riding the air currents brought a sudden realisation of why the name kite is so appropriate. They looked exactly like a group of children's kites circling overhead, their movement so imperceptible that they appeared to be controlled by strings operated from the ground. It is their distinctive forked tails that steer them, acting like the rudder of a boat, moving to the left and right causing them to dip, soar and circle. As they cruise their large wings move infrequently, just enough to give a little more power, a change of momentum. When they fly nearer the ground the undersides of their wings are clearly visible, patches of white against their darker body and wing tips, the dark parts more ginger than red. I stopped the noisy engine for a few seconds and could hear them calling, their shrill, 'Feeee fi fi fi,' echoing overhead. They are the most beautiful of birds, carrion feeders rather than hunters. My 1993 bird book says that they are a rare species and one blue blob in North Wales denotes the only place in Great Britain where they can be seen. Since the book was published a breeding programme started in Fineshade, an RSPB centre about twelve miles from here, and it has been very successful. The proof of this success now wheels above the fields. On this windy day it seems they have all come out to play. I am hypnotised watching them and at the next bend I run the boat aground. I eventually manage to pole off the mud, groaning, sweating and swearing. Above me the kites continued to soar effortlessly and unconcerned.

As we leave Wadenhoe, the spire to the right is the spire of the church at Achurch. There is a church at Achurch, nothing much else just a church. I like logical place names.

We go through the pretty lock at Lilford, past the elegant and impressive Lilford Hall and on to the lock at Upper Barnwell without incident. At Upper Barnwell there is a mill pond and a large old Mill that is now a hotel and restaurant. While I'm waiting for the lock to empty I wander over to peer in the window and look at the menu. It is tempting. Wouldn't it be lovely to moor up, remove the grime from under my fingernails, dress smartly and have a long leisurely lunch? I'll have the butternut squash risotto followed by the pan fried hake with beetroot and the lemon posset for dessert. But no time for that, I'm being shouted at to get on with raising the guillotine gate. Long leisurely lunches are out of the question when we have to get to the next mooring by dusk. No time to stop and look, far too busy, got to get moving, got to, 'Push On!' I couldn't have afforded those prices anyway.

Two locks further on, at Ashton, I glide on to the mooring and the wind whips me out again, after much fighting with the tiller trying to get into the right place my bow stuck on the lock gate and I could only get out by using the gate as a lever. I should have prayed that I hadn't damaged the lock but I only prayed that nobody had seen me damaging it, my image is far more important to me than the Environment Agency's lock gates.

The Fellow Traveller went into the next lock first and in view of the problems I was having with the wind decided to help. 'Throw me the centre rope,' he shouts. I threw him the centre rope, my nice long centre rope that was much more useful than his short one: easier to throw, more play when pulling the boat in. I sling it in the general direction of the bank miles away from where he stands. Unsurprisingly he failed to catch it and suddenly my engine stopped. After a few seconds of puzzlement as to why I should have ground to a halt realisation dawned that my nice long centre rope was now wrapped tightly around the propeller.

After a bit of trial and error with Stanley knives and carving knives and saws and wire cutters we find that the best implement to use to cut the rope is a bread knife. We manage to cut the rope above the water-line and release some of the pressure on the propeller. We get the boat through the lock and moored on the other side and then the serious business of unravelling the rope around the propeller started. The weed hatch is too deep in the bowels of the boat for podgy people like us to squeeze into so we take it in turns to lie on our stomachs and saw away at the ravel with the bread knife. Bits of frayed rope and curses float to the surface but the amount of rope around the propeller shaft doesn't seem to diminish. Aching shoulders and tired arms make progress slow. Fed-up with getting nowhere with the tangled mess of rope I try ringing boatyards to see if they had anybody who could help. This is very much a novice cry for help, experienced boaters would have just taken a fouled prop as an occupational hazard and got on with it. We didn't get any help though, all the boatyards seemed to be closed for the day. Nobody could come over from the canals until the following day. I have to admit that had it been the Fellow Traveller who had got his rope tangled in his propeller I would have been full of derision and spitting out acid comments about useless men but he wasn't handing out blame or pointing out my deficiencies, he just lay on his stomach and sawed away, relentlessly and totally ineffectually, at the ravelled rope. In the end we gave up trying to free it and moored at the lock for the night.

Early the next morning a narrow boat came along: seasoned boaters. They sympathised with my predicament and said they'd had everything tangled around their propeller shaft in their time, they said a nylon duvet cover was the worst to remove. They sympathised a bit less when they found it was my own centre rope that was tangled around my propeller. I was keeping quiet about that. I was just letting them assume it was a bit of old rope that I'd picked up along the way but The Fellow Traveller, honest to a fault especially when they were my faults, had to tell them the full story embellished with a few extraneous details about my girlie lack of ability to throw anything, especially ropes. Luckily the boat that had stopped was the one that, the day before, I'd moved off the last mooring space at Ashton for because we had only intended to stop for lunch and they'd wanted to stop overnight. He decided that one good turn deserved another even if the turns involved were disparate in time, energy and getting dirty. He stripped off his shirt, squeezed into the engine area and decided, after a trial with the Stanley knives and carving knives and saws and wire cutters that the bread knife was the best tool to use. He managed, after about fifteen minutes of hard labour, to release the propeller shaft.

What a hero. I'd have given him a hug and a kiss if he hadn't been covered in all the mud, oil and unspecified gunge from my bilges.

The boat and my saviour went on their way and I tidied up, put the boat back into a ship shape state and tied the shattered and frayed bits of rope back together again to produce one short and tatty centre rope. For a single handed sailor a centre rope is essential even a short, frayed, knotted one is better than nothing.

At the next lock I was very careful I came in slowly and gracefully but that was a waste of time. The wind was still pushing me out when I wanted to come in and pushing me in when I wanted to come out. It seemed to be changing direction just to annoy me. I've found this when I've been riding my bike. I go uphill against a head wind on the way there, stop have a cup of tea and a cake, look forward to an easy journey coasting home barely having to touch the pedals and come out to find that both the hills and the wind have changed direction and I have to engage first gear again to battle against the incline and the elements.

An Environment Agency worker doing something useful at the lock-side saw I was having difficulty mooring up and came to help.

I have already found that offers of help, with the notable exception of my recent hero, are often more trouble than they are worth. Men are always ready to spring to the aid of a woman making a dog's breakfast of handling a boat but they never ask if the aid they are about to give is the aid that is required.

All enthusiastically helpful men (I've never been helped by a woman) seem to push when you need a pull and pull when you need a push. They arrive, raise their hand in a manner that says, 'Don't worry your pretty little head about this, I have the matter under control,' then they push the bow out until they think it is in a satisfactory position and go on their way. I then have to spend another half hour extricating the boat from the position they have pushed it to.

One over helpful man at a lock, seeing me coast towards the lock landing to moor up jumped aboard and grabbed the bow rope and knotted it tightly round a bollard, waved cheerily and disappeared. He was smugly secure in the knowledge that he had been helpful to an inexperienced, woman boater. The only problem was that the bow was so tightly tied that the stern wouldn't come around and was ten feet away from the pontoon and if I was to step off, as I needed to, I would have stepped into the river. I then had to make a decision should I leave the tiller and untie the front end and hope we didn't go over the weir before I had chance to crawl back along the gunwale to the rear end or should I wait for help? In the end I waited for the Fellow Traveller to come round the bend and moor alongside so I could hold both boats and let him go and untie me. That meant he was pleased with himself for rescuing me. So in the depths of Northamptonshire there were two men feeling self-satisfied about rescuing a helpless woman. It was just a shame the woman hadn't needed any help in the first place.

So when the Environment Agency man on the lock-side offers to help I know I should simply say. 'Thank you but I can manage'. I don't say that because it sounds churlish and I have just been very grateful for some help from a passing stranger. I smile at him and he smiles back. I throw him the battered centre rope. He starts to heave me in. As I may have said before knot tying is not my forte. I could see the rope starting to unravel but before I can shout a warning it snapped apart. He fell over backwards. My first instinct is to laugh but I see that he is not in the least amused, understandably as he has just landed heavily on his coccyx on concrete. I stifle the laugh and apologise profusely shouting at the top of my voice above the noise of the wind and the roar of the weir that Rea and I are now drifting towards.

The boaters travelling downstream must have spread gossip about us because boaters coming upstream know who we are. It seems we are becoming well known on this stretch of the Nene. 'So you're the people who couldn't get the lock open.' 'You're the divorced pair that are travelling along together.' 'You're the woman who was screeching at the poor man on the other boat when he wasn't doing as he was told.' Now in the course of only an hour extra tales have been added, 'Ah, you're the woman that got her own centre rope tangled around her propeller.' and 'Are you the woman that put the poor Environment Agency man in hospital for six weeks?' The boats might move slowly but news on the river travels fast.

Towards Peterborough

We reached the safe haven of Fotheringay early in the afternoon and decide not to go any further, we still felt traumatised after all the drama with rope and propeller. We moored at the edge of a field where the impressive, truncated church of St Mary sat on a steep slope above the river. We'd been told that the farmer, the owner of the field, would arrive at 6pm clutching his treacle tin to collect his money. Sure enough as we are getting ready to head off for the mandatory evening drink in the village pub the farmer arrived with his Tate and Lyle tin clutched in his hand. We happily handed over the money, wishing more farmers along the Nene offered moorings in beautiful locations for four pounds a night because suitable mooring places along the Nene had been few and far between.

Fotheringay Church was a mine of information about Mary Queen of Scots who was incarcerated in the long demolished Fotheringay Castle before being tried and beheaded there. There was also a lot of information about Richard lll who was born in Fotheringay and, according to the Richard lll Society and contrary to what that nasty old Shakespeare said, was a jolly nice chap and beloved by all the peoples of the realm.

After drinks in the Falcon Inn we walked back to the boats by torchlight, through the churchyard and clambered through the gap in the church wall. It was a mild, starry night and there weren't any eerie screams or moans or headless queens wandering about. The only ghostly shapes were the faint outline of the sheep lurking in the misty field. The mound where Fotheringay Castle once stood and where Mary Queen of Scots lost her head sits darkly on the other side of the bridge. To say Mary Queen of Scots lost her head makes her sound as careless with her head as I am with my car keys. She had her head removed forcibly but evidently not very efficiently. One story is that the executioner missed the first time and split her head and needed another two attempts to sever her neck. When he grasped her hair to lift her head to show to the waiting crowds he held aloft a handful of wig and the head remained on the ground.

The next morning we are off again leaving the church on the mound behind us, then to the left of us, then behind us again until it eventually disappeared from view as we left Elton. Then the river meanders aimlessly through scenery and past the delightfully named Wansford in England. There was the odd sight of Thomas the Tank Engine heading over the bridge in our direction then I noticed we were passing Stibbington, where the Nene Valley Railway terminates. No time to moor up and wander around Wansford Station and look at the steam locomotives and old signal boxes or even to take a ride in the carriages pulled by Thomas because we still have to Push On! Especially as I have caused us to lose so much time by being careless with my centre rope. After Wansford the countryside started to lose its rolling aspect and flatten out in preparation for becoming the featureless, soggy landscape that is the Fens. We entered the chocolate box village of Water Newton, with its small but perfectly formed church surrounded by trees and flanked by stone cottages. The imposing water mill stands beyond the calm mill pond. Like most of the old mills on this stretch of the Nene it is bereft of its water wheel and has been converted, in this case to housing but it retains an impressive, 'I wonder what that was used for,' brick chimney in the garden.

The A1 follows the route of the original Great North Road which went through Water Newton. The A1 now passes within a few hundred yards of the village and the once busy Great North Road has become the quiet main street of the village. Any noise from the heavy traffic on the A1 is blotted out by the tumble of water flowing over the lock gates and the relentless cawing of the colony of rooks in the trees lining the river. Only a few hundred yards away runs one of the main arterial roads of the country yet down here on the river we seem to be in an isolated rural backwater.

The small, perfectly proportioned church that stands above the lock is Norman and named after St Remigius. I've never heard of a St Remigius. Who is this obscure saint and why is a church named after him? Although, as I don't have much more than a basic knowledge of saints, it is possible that St Remigius is a famous saint revered by many and has hundreds of churches throughout the land named after him.

I move away from Water Newton and a few hundred yards downriver I pass a man encouraging an excessive number of lithe, tan dogs to swim in the river. 'Lulu, wash your face, Mimi wash your face' he shouts at the two laggards who are hesitating on the bank. Lulu and Mimi reluctantly jump in the water, splash a bit and get out again quickly, shaking themselves dry. The rest of the pack swim and bounce around enthusiastically.

'What breed of dogs are they?' I shout to him.

'Hungarian Vizsla.'

'I've never seen them before.'

'They're very common in Hungary.'

If he's planning on breeding from this large pack they'll soon be very common here as well.

Pollarded willows stand in rows alongside a sluggish brook that trickles into the river. They are elderly trees, their trunks are wide, twisted and gnarled, topped with a green crew cut. In front of them there are younger, relatively newly planted willows resplendent with their brighter green crew cuts. The area beyond the stand of willows is a lumpy, bumpy tumulus which my map tells me is a bowl barrow dating from the Bronze Age.

According to my map the fields around this stretch of the river are awash with the sites of Roman villas, palaces and Roman pottery kilns. Just to the south of the river is the site of the Roman town of Dvrobrivae, where, in 1975, the country's earliest hoard of Christian silver was found. It is kept in the British Museum and is known as the Water Newton Plate. It is inscribed with names Publionus, Annicilla, Innocentia, Viventia, Roman names rather than Anglo Saxon names but still possibly inhabitants of this area. The Roman potteries along this riverbank produced high quality pottery called Castor ware, examples of which have been found throughout Europe. It is here that the old Roman Road, Ermine Street, crossed the Nene on its way from London to Lincoln and York. The Ermine Way is now the route for the A15 the dead straight road that makes up for its lack of bends by switch-backing over the hills of the Lincolnshire Wolds. Now, from my perch on the back boat, nothing of this Roman activity is visible all that can be seen is a scrubby nondescript field.

Standing on a low hill beyond the flood plain is the church at Castor. The tip of the steeple of the village church of St Kyneburgha is just visible through the trees. I remember visiting this church in a previous life. It stands on the site of the vast Roman palace which ceased to be occupied around 450AD. The only remains of the palace are the foundations jutting out of a wall opposite the church where Jacob sheep graze in the graveyard and a heavenly horde of 12th Century gilded angels hold up the roof of the Nave. There is a modern, wooden carved statue of the founder of the church, a Northumbrian princess named Kyneburgha who originally founded a monastery for both sexes on this site. The carving depicts a sweet little thing more Indian squaw than Northumbrian princess. I would imagine a medieval princess who founded a monastery was a lot tougher than she looks in the carving.

Within a square mile of this stretch of the river, on the edge of the uninspiring urban expansion of Peterborough, where a man walks a pack of Hungarian dogs and a jogger, plugged into his iPod, pounds along the bank there lies evidence of a millennium of habitation and industry and conflict. It is an ordinary landscape for ordinary people. It's not a landscape that speaks of the well-known historical names: Kings and Roundheads (Cromwell did a good bit of destruction in Castor), Roman Generals and Northumbrian Princesses may have lived and passed by here but this is a landscape that is redolent of the people that have worked here: the Roman builders who constructed the villas, towns and roads and worked the pottery kilns; the legions of foot soldiers who tramped past on their way to York; the workers that for centuries pollarded the willows for use in basket making and fencing; the farmworkers who tended the cows grazing in the water meadows; the millers who ground flour at Water Newton mill for over two hundred years. Even the name the Great North Road summons images from the earlier days of motoring when the man from the RAC, wearing large, white gauntlet gloves, saluted cars displaying the RAC badge.

I'd like to get off the boat and visit the churches and try to absorb the atmosphere of centuries of history; to walk over the tumulus and scrat around hoping to find long lost jewellery or weapons; to find shards of Roman pottery; to walk the route of Ermine Street and imagine the Roman legions passing through. But I can't because there is nowhere for me to stop. Officially I am allowed to moor on the banksides where there is a public footpath and as the Nene Way runs alongside this part of the river I would not break any rules and regulations by mooring up. But the bank is too rough to moor against. In the hollows the mud is glutinous and deeply pockmarked by the hooves of cattle coming down to the river to drink. The edge of the river is shallow and grounding is likely. From the back of the boat I can only look at the humps of the tumulus and at the pollarded willows and imagine the events that have taken place and the people that, over the centuries, have lived and worked here.

I progress downriver as it winds through trees and attractive parkland. Sculptures lurk amongst the trees but only these, and the number of people walking through the parkland, suggest that we are within the boundaries of a large city. The town of Peterborough arrives suddenly, the floodlights of the football club sprout on the right hand bank, the buildings of the city centre cluster on the left and the Cathedral sits squarely above them.

We both moor alongside a town park and settle down for the night across the river from a factory that works throughout the night. I lay awake listening to the screeching and wailing from behind its blank walls and the only explanation I can think of for the awful noise is that they are slaughtering cats.

Into The Fens

Somewhere in the early hours of the morning the factory must have run out of cats to slaughter, the noise stops and I manage a few hours of uninterrupted sleep but I still wake up in the morning feeling jaded. The tight knot of worry is once again sitting in my stomach. My map has a triangle with a red exclamation mark. A dire warning: 'Brigate Bend, the tightest dogleg in England.' It advises putting crew on the bank to warn of oncoming vessels. I haven't got a crew and Brigate Bend worries me. For the last few days I have added this particular worry to my general worries and this morning when I have to head off onto the Middle Levels, where the Brigate Bend is situated, my stomach is well and truly knotted. The Fellow Traveller isn't worried at all. He hasn't bothered getting any maps so is blissfully unaware of any of the hazards that lay ahead. I don't tell him about Brigate Bend, we'll see how he copes with it when he gets there.

It is once again sunny when we leave the moorings at Peterborough and pass through the manned Stanground Lock onto Whittlesey Dyke. Gradually I leave behind the housing estates and the urban detritus of squashed footballs, litter and half-submerged supermarket trolleys and head towards the chimneys of the brickworks in Whittlesey, the home of Brigate Bend. There's a sharp bend coming into Whittlesey that doesn't cause too many problems and I'm thinking the difficulty must be over-rated until I glance at my map and see I haven't yet reached Brigate. A road lined with houses runs alongside the river and the acrid smell of the brickworks floats on the breeze. The banks are high and hard and I wonder where I would have set my non-existent crew ashore, maybe they would have had to get off at Stanground and trot alongside me for six miles.

I approach the bend apprehensively. I have decided I will blow my horn to warn any on-coming vessels. I give two sharp blasts on the bilge pump. I really will have to remember which switch is which. I slow down coming into the bend, push the tiller far to the left, give a full rev, then as the momentum eases give a blast of reverse, back into forward and I'm round it in one smooth manoeuvre. What skill! Aren't I clever! Why did I spend so much time worrying? The Fellow Traveller is behind me, hidden from view by the sharp bend. I hear a sudden urgent revving of an engine, a thump of metal on concrete and a spate of bad language. Then the green bow crawls around the corner. 'That sharp bend was a bit unexpected,' he tells me, cheerily, when he pulls in next to me at the lock landing.

We go into the slow filling Ashline Lock at Whittlesey where the paddles, or penstocks as they appear to be called on the Middle Levels, need what feels like two thousand turns to raise. Once we leave the lock the Fellow Traveller steams on ahead leaving me alone in this flat landscape. I pass a fishing competition: fifty dogged anglers crouched in numbered slots along the bank. I proceed slowly trying to keep away from their lines and get one smile and wave and forty nine scowls. Kingfishers dart, flashes of turquoise and red amongst the bushes on the opposite side, the anglers probably don't like them either because they eat the fish.

Then it's further onto the Middle Levels system, an historically fascinating network of drains, pumping stations and sluices that stop the land from flooding. Most of the original drainage of the Fens was done over four hundred years ago by Dutch engineers, hand digging the waterways, meeting the wrath of the locals who felt their livelihoods of wild fowling, fishing and eel catching were being destroyed. The efforts of the Dutch completely changed the landscape, the courses of rivers, the lives of many and made fortunes for the few.

Crossing the Fens in a car you are conscious of endless earth and sky and telegraph poles; the dykes and drains and rivers are mostly hidden behind flood banks and buried amongst the greenery of the fields. When crossing the Fens by boat there comes the realisation that water, not earth or sky, is the natural element in this landscape. If it weren't for the intensive work of the Middle Level Commissioners who are responsible for Fen drainage in this part of East Anglia this dyke I am floating on would become a silted bog and the farmland would once more become waterlogged marshland. If global warming increases and water levels rise what is the future for this fertile, flat land? Will it eventually become uneconomical to drain and will the high yielding fields of wheat and vegetables once more revert to reeds and will the wildfowl flourish, or will our climate then be warm enough for them to become paddy fields?

On this Saturday in September the Fens are dressed in their Sunday best: vast blue skies interspersed with big comfy, white sofa clouds. Black, ploughed fields march away to infinity. A road runs for miles alongside the drain, an old farmhouse askew on its foundations leans towards the water, a tumbledown bridge threatens to fall on passing boats, skewwhiff telegraph poles dot the horizon. On a grey day this landscape is depressing, today the openness and emptiness and the sheer volume of clouds and sky is uplifting. Skeins of geese honk overhead and balletic wind turbines churn in the light wind. I chug along happily, sometimes feeling the drag of the shallow water, past reeds, bright flowers on the high banks, butterflies, dragonflies and damsel flies, alone in the flat landscape, relieved that Brigate Bend is far behind me.

At Floods Ferry, the dyke picks up the course of the Old Nene and runs on into March, past pretty gardens falling down to the river where boats are moored. Smells of BBQs, sounds of children playing, the river is alive with noise and activity, mooring spaces are difficult to find. This riverside March bears little resemblance to the dour Fenland town that I've often driven through and which must be still lurking somewhere nearby.

As I leave March the following day a man standing on a metal bridge shouts at me as I move towards it. 'Is that your boat?'

'Yes,' I say.

He moves to the other side of the bridge as I pass under it.

'Will you marry me?'

I laugh. I probably won't marry him but it was nice to be asked.

Then after straggling through the other side of March it's back to the wide, shallow drainage ditches and the wide skies. Signs direct us away from the wonderfully named Pophams Eau, which seems the most direct route and onto the narrow, shallow Well Creek. I wonder who Popham was and why his bit of ditch uses the pretentiously frenchified Eau and isn't named a Pophams Drain or Pophams Dyke or even Pophams Water.

Well Creek threads its way through the endless villages of Upwell and Outwell. The Middle Levels pamphlet warns boaters not to attempt to navigate Well Creek if ice is beginning to form because this makes the ice form unevenly and angers the locals who like to use the creek for ice-skating. At the first low bridge my tomato plant is knocked into the water, I'm so busy looking to see where it has fallen that my head nearly follows it, after that I get used to ducking down and steering the boat whilst squinting over the edge of the roof.

I have also been warned that it is a popular sport in Outwell for the locals to jump off one of the low bridges onto passing boats, run along the roof and haul themselves up at the next bridge. Today there are only a few elderly ladies walking alongside the river. I think I should be safe. They don't look the type to sling aside their shopping trolleys, sprint to the bridge and leapfrog over the parapet onto my roof. I could be wrong. Elderly ladies in these Fenland villages are somewhat unpredictable.

The mapmakers have forgotten to warn about the second sharpest dogleg in England. Coming out of Outwell there is an abrupt right hand bend. I negotiate it badly and end up flailing about in a willow tree, blinded, wondering what the front end of the boat is doing out of sight sixty feet ahead of where I'm struggling in foliage. I emerge, fortunate to still have both eyes intact, and find the bow heading towards a moored river cruiser. I take drastic evasive action, spin, hit the far bank and hear the scraping of paintwork at the front end and the clunk of the stern grounding. I pole off the mud and then check to see if anybody is watching. There are. Three grinning men, I can read their lips, 'Women drivers.' There wasn't a soul in sight when I completed a perfect corner at Brigate Bend but, of course, I always have an audience when I'm making a mess of things. Maybe I'm not as capable as I thought I was; maybe the learning curve is still steep.

I'd just been reading the book Waterlog by Richard Deakin about wild swimming. One of the places he'd swam was beneath the Mullicourt Aqueduct on Well Creek where he joined a group of local lads on a warm day in summer. Crossing the short aqueduct I look over into the water of the Sixteen Foot Drain. Even on a warm day in autumn it doesn't look a very tempting place to swim, the water is flat and grey and the banks steep and muddy. Today there is no sign of life, nobody daringly ignoring the Danger Deep Water signs or swimming lazily under the No Swimming signs.

I'm booked to go through Salters Lode Lock onto the short tidal stretch of the Great Ouse, at 3.30pm, the tide should have turned at 3.18pm but it's being awkward. There is a narrow boat lurched on the mud at the far entrance to the lock waiting for the water to rise. I sit chatting with the lock-keeper, looking over glistening mud banks. Lapwings pee-wit in the fields behind us and across the river a spume of slurry rises from a hidden tractor. As we wait for the water to arrive, I learn about both the predictability and the vagaries of tides, about spring tides and neap tides and how winds affect them and how a cruiser grounded under a bridge on the Old Bedford waiting for the tide to lift him may be waiting a long time. We're twenty miles from the sea at King's Lynn and this weak neap tide is taking its time getting here. Eventually it comes crawling in, edging over the mud flats, making a ripple on the glassy smoothness of the channel bringing with it the scent of the sea.

Leaving the lock I start to turn left and behind me hear a shout, 'Are you planning on going to Sweden?' I do a handbrake turn and go to the right, to Denver Lock and then onto the wide expanses of the Great Ouse where I can wave good-bye to The Fellow Traveller and head towards my winter home.

Winter

What made me think it was a good idea to live on a boat? Why did I think it was going to be a gentle, blissful experience? Which vengeful God decided to test my decision and my resolve by bringing forth the coldest, longest winter for thirty years?

I have to report that at the beginning of January the Revengeful God is winning hands down and my resolve has dissolved in the thin frosty air. And winter is only just getting into its stride.

One of the F.A.Qs' is, 'Is it cold in the winter?' Any seasoned live-aboard boater will reply, 'No. It's warmer than a house. It's toastie.' (toastie is a much favoured word amongst wintering boaters). Well all I have to say to the statements, 'It's warmer than a house.', 'It's toastie,' is Bollocks! I will repeat that. Bollocks! I'm cold. I accept that I may not have got the hang of keeping a boat 'toastie' but I used to have a draughty Victorian house and I managed to keep it a damn sight warmer than this lump of steel.

If the outside temperature hovers around zero I can keep myself and the boat warm but this winter it is hovering around -10 degrees and I can't. The whole business of living on a boat is not proving to be much fun. It isn't just the perpetual cold, the need to go to bed in ten layers of clothing and then, despite that, still wake up freezing cold with icicles on the end of my nose. It is also the hard work, the sheer physicality of the day to day living aboard a narrow boat in the winter.

My heating is a combination of gas central heating and a solid fuel stove. The gas cylinders, coal and wood had to be transported to the boat. I had to lift twenty five kilo bags of coal onto a trolley, and I am convinced that twenty five kilo bags of coal must be wrapped in a lead lined sack because they definitely weigh an awful lot more than twenty five kilos. Once the unwieldy trolley was loaded it had to be pushed through snow for miles and miles, negotiated down a steep runway which was always frozen and on which the trolley always skidded and threatened to drag us both into the marina. Then I had to unload the trolley. The nets of logs are not as heavy as the coal but they are an awkward shape and difficult to get through a narrow door. I used thousands of bags of coal and logs and was forever dragging them across the frozen wastes of the marina. And fires had to be mended and tended. Constantly. Turn your back for a few minutes, fall asleep in front of a glowing fire and it goes out and the temperature immediately plummets to below zero. When I had a good blaze going one end of the boat was on the point of melting and the other end still had frost on the windows so I had to put the central heating on as well to warm up the bedroom end of the boat. By itself the central heating warmed the bedroom, heated the water but had little effect on the living area.

When I put the central heating on it ate gas. That meant I had to change the cylinders approximately every half hour and the screw ends froze and I broke my nails and strained my back manhandling heavy cylinders in and out of the difficult to reach compartment in the bow. The bow cover was heavy and kept coming off its hinges and it's impossible to undo screws wearing gloves so they have to be removed and cold fingers hurt and everything is metal and fingers stick to frozen metal and when pulled off leave a layer of skin attached to the screw tops. I was grateful for my cratch cover it kept draughts out of the front door and it made a covered area where I could store coal and logs. Maybe the cratch cover can stay.

Water has to be drawn from a tap to fill the water tank. The nearest tap to the boat was leaky and dripped all over the pontoon and the water froze making the surface treacherous and getting in and out of the boat precarious. Re-winding the hose always seemed to mean getting soaked, making me cold and wet instead of just cold. Then the tap froze, which at least stopped it leaking but meant water had to be collected in containers from the tap inside the marina office. So water on board was rationed and I went swimming a lot so I could stand for hours under their hot showers and get clean and warm. I learned to wash in minimal amounts of water and recycle the contents of my hot water bottle. My hot water bottle became my new best friend.

And my feet were always cold, the floor of the boat is beneath water level and the water was frozen, therefore my feet were only a layer of steel and a bit of wood away from being immersed in blocks of ice. I wore so many pairs of thick socks that I could hardly walk, I sat with my feet on the hot water bottle, I wrapped my legs in blankets, I sat on the chair with my

106

feet in the air, I did star jumps along the corridor to try and improve my circulation but only succeeded in knocking the pictures off the walls. I ensconced myself in my sleeping bag and hopped from chair to kitchen to bathroom like a demented kangaroo or an over insulated contender in the mothers' sack race. Yet whatever I did my feet were always, always cold, painfully cold.

I wasn't a pretty sight: red-nosed, chapped lips, bleary eyed because of the smoke from the fire, nails encrusted with coal dust and knuckles grazed. I'd had to consume lots of comfort food so now the layers of fat sat under the layers of clothes and I resembled the Michelin Man. What's more I didn't care what I looked like. If my Fairy Godmother had arrived, complete with wand and offered me a sparkly ball gown and a chance to meet the man of my dreams she'd have been turfed out into the snow. I'd rather keep my scarf and gloves on and go to bed with a mug of hot chocolate and a hot water bottle. Dreams and handsome princes could wait until spring arrived.

The marina froze and the boat which usually moved didn't. When I first got the boat it was strange living in a home that swayed, when it became frozen into the marina it was equally strange living in a static boat. Walking along the boat made the ice creak and groan eerily. Because my car was a burnt out hulk in Northamptonshire I was without transport; it was too icy to get on a bike, and I had to walk for a mile and a half to buy provisions and then carry them back. I didn't want to buy lightweight salads, I needed potatoes and root vegetables and stodge so the load was heavy. I wondered if I was building impressive muscles but I wasn't going to take any of the layers of clothes off to have a look.

English winters are long and dark. When the marina froze it was impossible to get out to the pump-out station, which was situated on the riverbank, to empty the sewage tank. When there was a thaw snow melt turned the river into a savage torrent bringing debris and logs hurtling over the weirs. Attempting to get to the pump-out station was to risk being swept along a slalom course through the open locks out to King's Lynn and into The Wash. So the sewage was threatening to overflow and I had to instruct my infrequent visitors to empty their bladders and bowels before they left home.

I developed an affinity with Big Issue salesmen. I plumbed them for information about how to keep warm, how many pairs of socks it was possible to wear and still be able to walk, about the insulation properties of newspaper and cardboard. With my weekly purchase of the Big Issue (or sometimes twice weekly because I thought he deserved more custom) from the seller in Huntingdon Market Place I discussed the ambient temperature of today compared with yesterday, compared the warming properties of soup versus coffee, how his dog was coping with the cold and the Marshall Plan. Our discussions about the Marshall Plan where short lived, partly because of the cold but mostly because neither of us knew much about the Marshall Plan. It would start by him saying 'I think we could do to resurrect the Marshall Plan, do you know about the Marshall Plan?'

'Yes, it was something introduced after the war to help Europe.'

'It was after some war, not sure if it was the First World War or the Second.'

'I think it was the Second.'

'It helped France.'

'Or was it Germany?'

'Or was it all of Europe?'

'I think it was just the side that won.'

'To rebuild their armies.'

'Wasn't it to help their economies?'

'An American called Marshall thought of it.' Then an icy wind would blow and he'd retreat into a doorway and I'd scuttle off into a coffee shop determined to look up the details of the Marshall Plan on the internet but I always forgot. A few days later when I went back we had a bit of a conversation about the weather and how we'd managed to keep warm then he'd say, 'I think we should resurrect the Marshall Plan……..' and off we'd go again.

Perhaps I am over emphasising the hardships because it wasn't all bad, there are compensations when living on a boat in winter: the smell of wood smoke; a walk around the nature reserves leaving only my footprints on the pristine snow; watching the geese and birds gathering across the lakes; seeing the frost hanging heavy on the dead seed heads and grasses turning them into filigree sculptures; observing thin ice like finely woven lace form around the edges of frozen puddles; watching a red sun set behind stark trees. To go home to the hot glow of the stove and to the baked potatoes I'd left balanced on the fire bricks and the hot soup that I'd left simmering on the top. It smelt good and cooking on a solid fuel stove engendered a pioneering spirit.

Then there was the feathered variety of compensation. Each time I came through the marina gate I was met by three mallards, a duck and two drakes, they waddled down the pontoon after me and waited patiently outside for bread. I grew to love the aloof coots with their night-time screeching that echoed over the still waters and their over-sized knobbly, white, skeletal feet. Surely coots have the ugliest feet of all the river dwellers; they look as if they are wearing boots three sizes too big for them. Coots' feet always reminded me of being taken shopping for school shoes with my Mother. She always insisted that the shoes were, 'plenty big enough' so we bought over-large shoes and I slopped around in them for six months and by the time I'd grown into them they were worn out and we had to go and buy more shoes that were, 'plenty big enough'. That's what coots must feel like as they slop around with their big feet.

Every morning our resident heron stood on the opposite bank peering into the water looking for breakfast. I never saw him catch anything and as the water froze and the chances of him catching his breakfast became remote I was sure his expression turned from anticipation to plain puzzlement. One morning I woke to the breaking dawn turning the mist on the ice pink. Rising out of the pink mist two swans were standing on the ice and slowly spreading their wings it was an incredibly beautiful sight. But as the water of the marina froze more solidly the wildlife and the birds decamped to the still flowing river and the marina fell silent. The shrill night-time calls of the coots, the quacking of the mallards no longer echoed around the frozen water. The honks of the geese were only heard on their occasional fly pasts. Snow muffled footsteps and the hum of traffic on the roads was stilled. It was a cold, dark and silent world.

The best of all the compensations had nothing to do with the natural world. It was the local health club that had a swimming pool and a Jacuzzi and a steam room and a sauna and a bar. I could stoke the fire, put the hot water bottle in the bed and then go and sit in the Jacuzzi or steam room until closing time, get dried and dressed, then gallop around the perimeter of the marina, jump onto the boat (trying to avoid skidding on the ice) and dive into bed. Then I'd be snug until the early hours of the morning when the hot water bottle cooled off and the fire went out (I know a good stoker should be able to keep a fire going all night but that was something else I hadn't got the hang of) and the freezing temperatures penetrated the layers of bedding and clothing and I woke up with cold feet and a cold nose.

I was told there were people who were a lot worse off than me, the continuous cruisers were frozen into the canals many of them miles away from water and shops. It was pointed out to me that I was lucky compared to the earlier workers on the waterways who lived with their families on the canal barges year in and year out and if they wanted to earn any money had to ply their trade by breaking through the ice on frozen canals. They had to travel miles to get fresh water and food. They had small cabins with fires as their only source of heating and cooking and lived with their eight children their whippet and their granny all crammed together trying to keep warm and with only tea and bread and dripping to sustain them. They had to do the family wash in one old bucket full of cold water. They didn't have a nearby health club with a Jacuzzi they could jump in and warm up. I was just being a moaning, centrally heated conditioned softie who didn't appreciate how hard life was or had been for the previous denizens of the canals.

It doesn't help to be told there are, or had been, people worse off than yourself especially when the person telling you how lucky compared with others is living in a large warm house with a car parked outside and a supermarket across the road. If one is comparing oneself to anybody we make comparisons with people better off than us, that's how advertising works. We want what they've got. Saying I am lucky compared to long dead bargees is the equivalent of my mother telling me to be grateful for my plate of over-cooked sprouts because there are starving children in Africa, or that my feet may be cold but I'm not as unfortunate as Arctic explorers who lose their toes because of frost bite. I replied, in no uncertain terms, that I had been brought up in the frozen north in a house that was heated by one small coal fire around which we all huddled causing us to have red faces, mottled legs and freezing backs. We didn't remove our liberty bodices from November to March in case hypothermia set in and in the morning we had to chip the ice from around the bedroom doors if we wanted to get out. I'd experienced chilblains. What is more I'd just lived in the Philippines where I'd had to carry all my water from the tap in the yard to the bucket in the bathroom, no hot running water there mate, just a big bucket and a scoop and I had to scrunch my way through cockroaches to get to the bathroom in the first place. I'm not a centrally heating conditioned softie, I'd known hardship. I know life can be tough. I'm not a wuzz.

At the beginning of February more of the same weather was forecast, my water tank was empty and my sewage tank was full so I flew out to the heat and sun of Kenya to visit friends. I stayed a month.

I kept a watch on the UK weather, noticing with glee that it was still cold and snowy. I emailed photos back home of me on a beach, in a bar drinking cold beer, on safari in the hot African sun with simple comments like, 'I hear it's still snowing there,' or 'I bet you'd like some of this sunshine,' or 'I hope you're keeping as warm as I am.'

When I arrived back from Kenya the road to the marina was flooded and I had to wade through icy water to reach the pontoons. The boat was cold and unwelcoming. Something had leaked and I had a soggy carpet and the air was heavy with dampness and the smell of mildew. The gas and electricity had to be switched back on, the batteries recharged and the fire lit. I'd drained the water so the tank had to be re-filled before I could have a coffee or put the central heating on or warm up in the shower. I'd become acclimatised to temperatures of twenty eight degrees and days of bright sunlight and had forgotten how drab are rainy days and how miserable it is to be cold. In addition my friends had taken umbrage at all my cheery emails and photos showing Kenyan sun whilst they were battling with a severe English winter and none of them were speaking to me. And I've come home to the worst news of all. Winter may be still in full flow but my winter membership of the Health Club had expired and I couldn't go and warm up in the Jacuzzi without paying a fortune for an annual membership.

Huddled in coat and gloves and scarves I looked out at the grey water and the leaden sky I wondered what on earth had made me think that it was a good idea to live on a boat. Living on a boat was a miserable, cramped, uncivilised form of existence. I was homesick. My boat was my home and I was sick of it.

I made a firm decision to put the last six months down to experience, to sell the boat and buy a well-insulated, centrally heated semi where I can have a long hot bath, where I can invite more than two people to dinner at a time or even hold a party, where I could get a cat just for the pleasure of swinging it. My cosy semi is going to be as far away from rivers and canals as possible. I was never, ever again going to set foot on any type of boat. Never, ever.

Spring

The calendar says that Spring is officially here. I'm looking forward to sailing away and cruising through the waterways of England. I have a plan. I've spent many a dark evening with the maps spread on the floor in front of the fire trying to decide where I want to go. Now I have decided. The plan is that I will leave the safe harbour of the marina on the 1st April, maybe not the most auspicious of dates but probably a suitable one in my case. I will go to St Ives for a day or so then onto Cambridge stay a few days around there seeing friends and family then move off towards Ely. When the weather forecast is clement I will retrace the route I took last autumn and head off onto the canals. Once on the canals I'll motor on towards Wales, loop around there for a while and then find somewhere to stay for the winter.

The weather hasn't looked at the calendar and doesn't know that it should be spring. The cold days linger on. Then as the days gradually grow longer the weather becomes marginally milder and there is a faint haze of green on black branches then a flush of pink appears at intervals amongst the stark bushes. We slowly crawled into the season of yellow flowers and green shoots, of lightness and fresh smells, of blossoming and renewed growth. And on the water there was violence and rape.

The swans were one of the first perpetrators. They

did a few beautiful balletic dances with elegant neck interlocking and a graceful flapping of wings. That got the niceties out of the way and then it was down to business. It's grab the woman by the neck until she has a look of abject misery in her beady black eyes, dunk her head in the water so she is unable to protest and then have your evil way with her. When she is on the point of asphyxiation let her go, then flap around a bit, stretch the wings, dip under the water a few times then settle down and live happily ever after with the victim and your brood of grey cygnets.

The worst offenders are the mallards because they go in for gang bangs. The marina is alive with the sound of squawking and splashing as gangs of drakes chase a lone duck through water and reeds and bushes, across the grass into the water. She mostly runs or swims, rarely does she try to escape by flight. The pack of five or six drakes follow on, it sometimes resembles an episode of the Keystone Cops or the Benny Hill Show but the outcome isn't funny for the hapless duck. Once she is caught the drakes hold her by the neck and each take their turn with her. I've heard the death rate among ducks is high which could account for the dearth of mature females and predominance of males and the continuing trend towards gang rape. The female is then left to bring up her indeterminately fathered, brood alone. At least the swans for all their boorish behaviour are good fathers and take their responsibilities seriously. Male mallards just abandon their mate, go scrounging for bread and leave the female to cope as a single parent. They're the webbed feet equivalent of the absentee, irresponsible father that politicians and the tabloid press rant about.

I bask in the first warm sunshine of a blossoming spring and prepare the boat ready to leave. I check the oil and water, do a bit of polishing. My sister is coming to stay for the week so the revised plan is that she will crew me down to Cambridge and then she will catch the train to Stansted for her flight back to Italy leaving me alone to turn around and head canalwards. In the days prior to her arrival winter returns and it rains heavily and non-stop. The Environment Agency closes the river to all traffic. Strong Stream notices are posted, sluice gates and lock gates are opened to allow water to drain down from the upper reaches of the river and prevent flooding. Milton Keynes, Bedford and St Neots may have dry feet but all the water being pushed down has washed my plans away. I go and check on the river regularly, the only items moving across the surface are logs and branches and six orange life-belted canoeists getting a rare Great Ouse based opportunity to practice white water rafting near tumultuous weirs. The river is high and there is little room for movement under low bridges. The flow is strong and there is much rubbish in the water and that could snag the propeller. I won't be going anywhere until the waters subside.

By the time my sister arrives I have accepted that there is no chance of moving the boat for a number of days. She doesn't care. She has got a bad chest infection and she doesn't want to go anywhere. I drag her out for a few muddy walks but really all she wants to do is sit by the fire and cough. After a few days the river starts to go down and the wind starts to come up. On the last day of her visit the Strong Stream notices have been lifted and it's bright and sunny but very breezy. I make an, 'It's now or never,' decision and say that afternoon we will go to St Ives. She coughs a lot and looks pained but the decision is made, we're moving. I have a feeling that her illness has been exaggerated so she can stay warmly in bed whilst being provided with a constant supply of tea, toast and books to read. I decide a windy day spent operating locks will do her the world of good.

Apart from the odd spin around the marina and onto the river to visit the pump-out station it is five months since I've driven the boat. I'm apprehensive and fumbling and trying to work out how to get out of a tight space, turn in a tight space and leave the marina without demolishing the line of fibre glass cruisers moored behind me. I reverse as far as I can and put the boat into neutral, then slip on the wet surface of the deck, make a grab for something to halt my fall, find the accelerator handle and fall on it pushing it hard into full forward revs. The boat roars forward towards the pontoon. I manage to right myself, grab the wildly swinging tiller and turn it although not before the boat smacks into the stanchion holding the pontoons. The boat bounces off and I struggle to control it, it's heading in the wrong direction and for a few moments I have a vision of writing off a million pounds worth of moored fibre-glass cruisers. Somehow I straighten the boat, sling it back into reverse to slow it and when it is steadied and slowed I plod towards the turning point.

Luckily the only consequences are a dent in the stanchion and my wildly, palpitating heart.

My sister pops up in front of me, pale-faced, wide-eyed, still coughing, 'Did you mean to do that?' she asks.

The river is high and the current is running fast and it is windy but I manage to get into Brampton Lock without any difficulty. At the same time a party of walkers is resting on the lock bridge watching my flawless entry into the narrow space with admiration.

'Oh you can tell she knows what she's doing,' says a man in an orange anorak with a plastic coated map around his neck. I smile and preen and wave majestically to them but I should know better because anybody saying, 'She knows what she's doing,' is the kiss of death and it ensures that I will make a complete mess of the next manoeuvre.

I come out of the lock to make a sharp right turn into the channel and away from the mill pond that leads to a weir. Even on the best of days it is a difficult turn for a sixty foot boat to manage and, in mitigation, I will repeat that there was a strong current and the wind was blowing onto my bow. Ten minutes later the engine was still roaring and my arms were aching and I'd been going backwards and forwards between the weir and the lock and still been unable to turn the bow through a ninety degree angle. The nearest I'd come to getting around the corner onto the river channel was to nearly uproot the oak tree which has stood on this spot for centuries and was getting in my way.

The group of walkers on the lock bridge were still

there; watching, entertained. Any expressions of admiration had long since left their faces and I didn't hear anyone else say, 'She knows what she's doing.'

I did eventually get round that corner and we did eventually reach St Ives and I felt as exhausted as if I'd travelled to the North Pole and back rather than just moved a few miles downriver.

The next day my sister flew back to Italy but she kindly left her chest infection behind so I could get the full benefit of it. Presumably she wanted to prove it hadn't just been a ruse to get attention and waitress service.

I left St Ives a few days later to move towards Earith and then onto Cambridge. The river was still high and was over the banks and onto the flood meadows, making it difficult to tell where the river ended and the banks started. I had visions of running aground and being stranded in the fields until the following winter but I managed to negotiate it safely, went through the lock and down the Old West River.

The sun was shining I was handling the boat successfully. At last I was on my way.

At The Doctors

You do feel a pillock when you lose a boat. I was in full control when I came into moor against a riverbank at Stretham. I stepped off neatly with the rope in one hand and the mallet and mooring pin in the other. I pulled Rea in, bent to start hammering the mooring pin into the ground and then a sudden blast of wind took hold of her and pushed her away from the bank. I pulled hard on the rope but the wind was stronger than me. It got to the point where I had the option of letting go or landing in the river. Somewhere at the back of my mind must have been the memory of punting down the Cam when the pole got stuck in the mud and the punt started to drift away and I had to make the decision to stay with either the punt or the pole. I made the unwise decision of staying with the pole. This time I made the rather more sensible decision to let go of the rope and stay with the bank. I watched Rea drifting away in the wind until she was pinned to the opposite bank, seventy feet away with the ropes trailing wetly in the water.

I stood there, bemused, wondering how I was going to get my home back. Then from river cruisers moored in front and behind people came running. Why couldn't they have come running two minutes earlier when I really needed them? They seemed to find my predicament amusing. If it had happened to somebody else I'd have found it amusing but it had happened to me so I couldn't see what was so funny about having my boat marooned on the opposite bank. I just felt a pillock.

Once their jokes had petered out and their amusement had subsided they decided that one of them would take me across to Rea, we would be happily re-united and I could drive her back and they would help pull her in and moor her up properly. So the two men and I got onto one of the cruisers and the wind whipped it rather too smartly across the river and bumped it into the side of Rea and I climbed on board, very clumsily because I wasn't used to moving around the decks of cruisers and they appeared to be even more difficult than narrow boats. The spare man came on board with me and with much pushing with poles and revving of engines and burning of diesel and getting out of the reeds and being pushed back into the reeds by the wind we eventually managed to get back to the other side of the river. The men on the bank grabbed the ropes and pulled and the wind gusted and suddenly they were straining for all they were worth to hold the boat. I was glad about that because I wouldn't have liked it to be too easy for them. I wanted them to know that it was difficult to pull in a narrow boat against the wind and it wasn't just being a weak and feeble woman when I had to let go.

I got the impression that my dilemma had proved a bonding experience for the crews of the cruisers for they stayed on the bank and gossiped until dusk fell and they were joined by the crews of two other cruisers that came in to moor. The noise of the wind abated and was replaced by gales of laughter from the little group. They were laughing at me. I just know they were laughing at me. I went to bed early and stuck my head under the duvet but I could still hear them laughing at me.

I didn't feel like getting up early the next morning, I didn't feel well but neither did I fancy facing the spectators of my losing battle with the wind so I crawled out of bed just after a calm and sunny day dawned. I left Stretham not long afterwards, sneaking away as quietly as a narrow boat with a noisy engine could manage.

I reached Clayhithe mid-morning. Hithe or Hythe means a landing or a dock. Was this where the clay was loaded in bygone days? It was only a passing thought. I didn't feel well enough to really care about the origin of the name because the family chest infection had become well embedded and I was coughing ferociously and my chest hurt. I was beginning to think I should have offered a bit more sympathy to Marcelle. Maybe her illness was genuine and not just an excuse to lie in bed reading all my books and expecting tea and toast and sympathy.

Friends who came aboard to lunch decided I was going to the doctors the next day and they would come over and pick me up. I am close to where I used to have a warm, centrally heated house with running water and an electric supply that doesn't rely on batteries being re-charged and a sewage system that didn't need pumping out at smelly sanitary stations so I was still registered with the local doctor's surgery. I like the doctors and should I be seriously ill I'll be referred to Addenbrookes Hospital which is one of the best in the country and as I've friends and family in the area I have places to stay should I need to visit the doctors. I intend to remain registered with this surgery. The receptionist has other ideas.

'Miss Green we've had mail returned marked, 'No longer at this address, could you give me your new address?'

'I haven't really got an address, I live on a boat and it moves I can give you my daughter's address as a contact.'

'Where does your daughter live?'

'London.'

'So you'll be living there and registering with a local doctor.'

'No, I'll be living on the boat not in London.'

'Well if your official address is in London, you'll have to go to a doctor in London.'

'Well then I'll give you the address of some friends who live locally, they won't mind accepting my mail.'

'Will you be living there?'

'No I'll be living on the boat.'

'Well we can't accept that, you have to live in the area before we can keep you on our list.'

'But I move the boat, do I have to register with a doctor every time I moor up?'

'I don't know but if you don't live in this village anymore you can't be registered with this doctor. You can see him now but after that you will have to register with the doctor nearest where you are living.'

'But where I am living changes every day.'

She gives me a look that says, 'Well that's your problem.'

'You've told me to register in London where I don't live so why can't I stay registered here where I don't live either?'

A queue had formed and at first they'd been interested in the discussion but, due to the lack of gory medical details or fascinating personal insights, they were rapidly becoming bored and restive. After another few more minutes of circuitous conversation about where I was not living, to the background of coughs, shuffles and impatient sighs, it was decided I could use my ex-neighbours' address and stay registered at this surgery for the time being. So I saw the doctor and got prescribed antibiotics for the chest infection and had tests on some funny stomach problem I'd been having.

I am officially a person of No Fixed Abode. Being of No Fixed Abode has its advantages. I don't have to pay Council Tax. I don't get Census Forms to fill in. If I had a television (I don't) I should have a TV Licence but very few boaters bother with licences as there are few, if any, detector vans roaming around the rivers and canals. A driving licence is more problematic as the DVLA insist on a residential address before they issue a driving licence, a Poste Resante or forwarding address is not sufficient. Pension and benefit payments can be dependent upon a fixed address. If I'm having difficulty registering with a doctor how much more difficult is it for the truly homeless? I can use friends' and families' addresses for registrations and for post to be forwarded to but when you have lost contact with family and your only friend is the one living next to you on a park bench then what do you use as a permanent address?

Cambridge

Across the parapet of the bridge a daub of white paint says, 'Queens'. I must be heading towards a centre of academic achievement if the graffiti is ugly but the apostrophe is in the right place.

Reaching the outskirts of Cambridge there's a flash of turquoise and red, the first kingfisher I've seen this year. This is followed by the first scull, and the first university eights. A smart grey narrow boat moored at the edge of a manicured lawn has a large sign saying, 'Rowers keep your oars off the paintwork'. This owner's contribution to the acrimony between Town and Gown, rowers and boaters, river cruisers and narrow boats and, of course, the anglers who hate anybody who disturbs the fish on the patch of river in which they are dangling their hook and line.

On the outskirts of Cambridge there is a stretch of bankside known locally as the railings. The road runs alongside the river for a few hundred yards, white railings stop pedestrians falling into the water. A variety of boats are tied up to the high railings. I understand there is a dispute as to who is responsible for this stretch of the bank of the Cam, Cambridge City Council or South Cambridgeshire County Council, so a motley collection of boats and their owners have taken advantage of this dispute and have moored here free of charge and free of fear of being moved on. There are regular protests from the residents in the houses along

Riverside, regular moans to the council about this community that are perceived as waterborne Travellers, itinerants outside the scope of council tax, drug users and general undesirables. One or two of the boats are well kept, others resemble floating skips and look as if they are about to sink, most of the others fit somewhere in the middle of this spectrum. There is a long waiting list for an official mooring in Cambridge. Getting a rented property is difficult and expensive, house prices are high. For the residents of these boats this is probably their only chance of living in Cambridge where they may be near work, friends and family. There is a strong scent of privilege and entitlement from the colleges and science parks and from the rowers on the river in Cambridge. Maybe it is good that there is some counter-balance to this by the more human smells emanating from this stretch of river.

I'm gliding past the boathouses opposite Midsummer Common when a learner boat of coxed eights suddenly pushes off the bank in front of me only noticing sixteen tons of steel bearing down on them when I blow the horn. I sling the boat into reverse gear but it's obvious I'm not going to be able to stop on a sixpence so they go into panic mode. An octopus of oars flails in all directions as they spin towards my bow. The cox bellows instructions and seconds before being mowed down they co-ordinate their oars and shoot across the river crashing into the far bank. An experienced eights smirk their way past at ninety miles an hour producing more wash than the Queen Mary in full steam.

I moor at Jesus Green next to a group of homeless people. I tell a friend later that they can't be drunk because they were only drinking lemonade but from the look on her face I think I'm being a bit naive about the contents of the lemonade bottles. I go for a wander around Cambridge returning four hours later to find they are still there. As I'm climbing into the boat the only woman in the group shouts, 'Hello darlin, do you mind if I sit on your roof?' I show her the stirrups to use to climb onto the roof. I don't want her damaging the paintwork. 'That's OK,' she says and sort of neatly back flips onto the roof.

'I wish I could get onto my roof like that.' I say.

'Yeah, well you're old and a bit fat so you couldn't manage it,' she replies.

When I leave later to go to the shop for some food I see she's been joined on the roof by a young man with the glazed opaque eyes and the intermittent teeth of a perpetual drug user. 'I've told him to be careful of your paintwork,' she says.

'Your roof needs some painting,' he tells me, 'I used to be a car paint sprayer, I'll borrow stuff and do it for you if you like.' The 'borrowing of stuff' sounds a bit dodgy to me but I don't like to say that. I just make noises about only being allowed to moor here for 48 hours so wouldn't be here long enough for the borrowing of the stuff and the painting of the roof to occur.

I decide it's best to stay friends with the locals so working on the same principle explorers used when taking beads for the natives I buy some food for them.

I'm not very generous though, after all their palates are probably shot with all the alcohol and drugs they take, I get cotton wool bread, plastic cheese and chicken slices past the sell by date and make a large plate of sandwiches for them. Later, I notice the older man feeding the sandwiches to the ducks and it dawns on me that they probably get the leftovers from Pret a Manger and are more used to crayfish, avocado and smoked salmon than the manky cheese and dodgy chicken that I've just given them.

Late in the evening three more boats arrive, they have resident permits but have been moved from their sites along Midsummer Common because of an impending University Regatta. They tie up alongside each other three deep because the visitor moorings are now full. 'Fucking University' one of them says, 'Think they own the place, they say jump and expect everybody else to say how high.'

The following morning the crews that are taking part in the regatta are out practising. Rowers get up early. It's only six o'clock and there is a lot of splashing and voices outside my bedroom window. The boat rocks violently, the crew of the eights boats manage to produce a great amount of turbulence even when they are hardly moving.

They have to turn just outside my boat. I hadn't realised, until I watched learner crews perform, how difficult it is to co-ordinate the turning (or spinning to use the correct term) of a multi-crewed boat. I feel a thump followed by scraping and bumping. 'Just use your oars to push off from the side of that boat.' I hear a vertically challenged cox shout. 'Those barges shouldn't be allowed along here anyway.' The animosity felt by the rowers towards the boaters is alive and well and afloat at 6am on a May morning. Fucking University they think they own the place.

I'm leaving the boat the next morning when I hear a yell from the footpath at the top of the bank. 'Morning darling.' It's my friendly drunk from the previous day, I wave. 'I'm coming to see you later,' she shouts. And she does. For the next few days that I overstay the forty eight hours mooring limit, Kim (we are formally introduced later) and a sundry collection of friends take up residence on my roof. Sometimes I find the rocking of the boat as they get on and off irritating, and the drunken arguments can be disturbing yet somehow I feel safe knowing they are above me and miss them when at about 10pm they disperse for the night.

I'm introduced to Kim's sister ('She's not an alchi like me.'), told her worries when her man is hauled off to hospital and admitted to intensive care with a perforated ulcer (he's back two days later drinking cans of Special Brew) and meet Casper, a smiley dog with a bent waggy tail. I become attached to this small friendly, wayward community who care for each other. When I knock my bucket and sponge into the river I have six drunks forming a chain to try and retrieve them.

Mooring in a city is a different experience to mooring out in the countryside. Bird watching is replaced by people watching. An elderly couple wearing matching white hats sit in identical poses, hands on knees, heads moving in unison, monitoring the flow of bikers, joggers and tourists. They look like a pair of umpires at Wimbledon following the play.

The sound of a child's tantrum is magnified by the water and passers-by stop and look thinking she is being, at the very least, murdered.

A university contingent string nets across the water, 'Doing a fish count,' they say when asked.

A rowing boat in Cam Conservators green livery passes laden with bikes covered in drying mud and slimy green weed. 'Here, bring my bike back' one of the homeless shouts across the river. The Cam Conservators man laughs and waves.

A Cam Conservators inspector stops outside my boat to phone his boss 'They haven't got a licence to fish... No.. No.. Well they're drinking but they're not really drunk. No they were perfectly polite ... it's just if they get really drunk they'll start throwing maggots at rowers and falling in the river.'

The tour boat Georgina goes past rocking my boat violently. The Japanese tourists on board are absorbed in an English cream tea ceremony.

A young girl dressed as Snow White stands on the lock side next to the sign that says, 'Don't feed bread to the wildfowl' and feeds bread to the ducks.

A resident boater comes along to ask me my opinion on the City Council plan to move the visitor moorings beyond the lock where there are now residential moorings. She says the council have told her it is because, 'Boaters like going through the locks'. Seeing as the council have frequently made attempts to ban all boats from the riverbank I can't imagine they suddenly decided to make the life of visiting boaters more joyful by encouraging them to use Jesus Lock. Later, I read a notice on the bridge which says they are attempting to re-locate the visitor moorings because the lock is used so infrequently it is silting up and a regular passage of boats through the lock should clear it out.

A photographer asks if she can photograph me on board my boat for a project she is working on recording the lives of people living on boats in Cambridge. I check her web-site later (suzanne.middlemass.co.uk) but my picture doesn't appear despite my best attempts to stand in a position to show Rea at her best and to arrange my face into that of a fascinating and unusual person. We must have both been decreed too ordinary to appear on the website.

Two friends arrive bearing ice-cream. We sit in the bow licking our dribbling cornets and watch the eights spinning their boats; it's a good spectator sport and we discuss the relative skill of each crew. My friend suggests we put numbers on cards and give them scores for style and technical merit. It seems a good idea and it amuses us but it's a warm day and we can't be bothered to get up and look for pen and paper.

A fire engine stops on Jesus Green and three firemen in bright yellow wetsuits, red life jackets and yellow helmets get into the river. At first I think they are looking for something, it was only a few days ago that a body was removed from the river above the weir but it soon becomes apparent that it is only a training exercise. At a shouted instruction they lie on their backs and float in the river. A line is attached to a similarly clad woman and she swims out to them, the instructor yelling at her to approach them from upriver.

'Are you going to attempt resuscitation?'

'No they're dead.'

'How do you know they're dead?'

'They've just told me.'

The exercise over they pull the rescuer out and the three dead bodies stand up in the river and walk towards the bank.

I wave to a friend in an eights boat she ignores me but a complete stranger in another boat waves back enthusiastically.

Rain suddenly hammers on the roof. Jesus Green and the footpath along the river empty magically. The homeless leave my roof and take shelter under a tree and a straggle of tourists crossing the iron bridge put up a kaleidoscope of umbrellas. Large raindrops dance across the river making intricate patterns on the water; they bounce off the surface and fragment into tiny sparkling diamonds. Watching rain on water is as hypnotic as watching the reflections of the sun or of the moon on the water. Only rain is colder and wetter so after a while I stop leaning out of the hatch, close it and go inside the boat listening to the rhythm of the rain on the roof, the swish of the tyres on the wet tarmac of Chesterton Road and the drone of the weir.

Stop Press
Lunching Ladies Save a Drunk from the Drink

Three middle-aged ladies were having a late lunch on board a narrow boat moored in Cambridge when they became aware of an altercation taking place between some men. They had noticed that one of the men had been sitting on a park bench for a few hours sharing bottles of strong cider with a blonde woman. Another two men arrived and an argument broke out. One of the new arrivals started swinging punches at the man on the bench. The man on the bench didn't retaliate only backed away, this situation continued for a few minutes before the new arrival grabbed hold of the other man and threw him in the river. The two recent arrivals and the woman then left leaving their victim in the water.

The three women on the boat reluctantly left their half-eaten lunch and strolled over to help the drowning man.

Stephanie Green said, 'I grabbed the boat hook in case I needed to haul him out. I had done a life-saving course but this was many years ago and I had only saved a brick from the bottom of a swimming pool not a drunk from the bottom of the river. I seemed to remember that when diving in to save a life it is essential to wear pyjamas but I didn't have time to put them on.'

Marcelle Green said, 'I told the other two if he

needed mouth to mouth resuscitation I wasn't going to do it.'

Chris Castle said, 'When we reached him he was holding onto the ropes of a boat. I asked if he could swim and he said he couldn't so I told him in that case he better not let go of the ropes. I suggested that he move over to the back of the boat where he could climb on the ledge and get out but he said he'd broken his ribs and just wanted to rest for a few minutes.'

Stephanie Green reported that after some time the man decided to try and get out. Keeping hold of the rope he lifted his legs on to the bank but this tipped him over and his head started to disappear under the water. One of the women grabbed a leg and the other two grabbed an arm each and they managed to pull him out.

The ladies were asked if they offered to call an ambulance or send for medical assistance. They said no they just left him on the bank to dry off and went back to their lunch, they felt that they needed a large glass of wine each after all that drama.

Stephanie Green did say that she thought of taking him a mug of hot sweet tea but he did look rather unhygienic and she didn't want to risk contaminating one of her best mugs.

Mr Asbo

Mention to anybody living in Cambridge that you're living on a boat that is currently cruising on the River Cam and the first question they ask is, 'Have you met Mr Asbo?' Mr Asbo is a local celebrity; he's featured in the local press, national newspapers and has even appeared on television. There have been appeals to The Queen about Mr Asbo because as he is one of her subjects it was felt she may take a personal interest. Mr Asbo is a swan.

Swans will attack dogs and people and itinerant wildlife when they are protecting their nests and their young. Mr Asbo has become famous because he does it with more determination, gusto and bloody mindedness than other swans. He has raised the natural aggression of the species to new heights. He attacks sculls, rowing boats and dinghies. He attacks anglers, dogs and dog walkers and babies in prams. They don't have to be near his nest, he'll cross the river and go to great lengths to get at them. He flies in to attack eights aiming his most deadly attacks at the cox. He may have a brain the size of a pea but he's worked it out that it's best to attack the small, unarmed one at the back of the boat.

The stroppy swan has a protector, a man moored on the bank at Stourbridge Common known as Battleship Bob, who regularly berates anybody trying to fight back when they are attacked. He is said to be even more belligerent than his feathered friend. On the other hand Bill Keys, president of Cambridgeshire Rowing

Society, has applied to the Queen to have the dastardly swan removed from the river. I have no idea where he wants him removed to but as long as his precious rowers are safe he probably doesn't care. So the swan soap opera goes on and on and keeps the residents of Cambridge amused unless, of course, they are the ones being attacked by the fearless feathered fiend.

At this juncture I have to say that since I've lived on the river my opinion of swans has changed. I used to think of them as beautiful and graceful, sweet natured, bread guzzling creatures I now think they are bad-tempered, vindictive, vicious creatures and every one of them deserves to receive an Asbo. On my list of favourite river dwellers they languish near the bottom. They're just above anglers and the reason they haven't been placed lower is that they are undeniably beautiful and graceful, something that can rarely be said about the anglers.

One afternoon I sat on the bow reading a book and suddenly felt a pain in my arm. A swan trying to get my attention had taken a large bite. In reaction I smacked him on his neck with my book but he wasn't intimidated he just ruffled his feathers and hissed at me. I moved away.

To see two swans fighting over territory is potentially to see a fight to death. When one gets the upper hand and is holding his opponent's head under water bankside spectators start throwing stones to try and make the victor let go. I don't join in I'm more inclined to think of two fighting swans in the same way I think of two overpaid, bad-tempered, contenders at

Wimbledon. I'd like them both to lose.

The swans on the river are Mute swans. Mute swans are the couch potatoes of the swan world. They are resident on these waters not like their relatives the Whooper and Bewick swans who winter nearby on the Ouse Washes. The Bewick and Whooper swans fly in from Scandinavia and Iceland. The Whoopers are renowned for being the most aggressive breed of swans, Mr Asbo would be a pussycat compared to the standard Whooper swan. They spend the summer in Iceland then have a continuous flight of around fifteen hours to cover one thousand two hundred miles at heights of nine thousand metres in sub-zero temperatures. If you can manage a journey like that, bringing the wife and young children along as well, then I think you're entitled to a bit of bad temper. The Mute swans on the other hand have just spent their lives gliding around on rivers and lakes being protected by the Queen and fed by an admiring public. They should be grateful for their easy existence and be more polite to their neighbours and benefactors.

Now I've spent time on the river and had a chance to watch the behaviour of the wildlife at closer quarters my opinions about many of the other river dwellers has also changed. I could now watch the herons forever yet when I lived in a house I had sympathy with a neighbour whose expensive Koi carp were frequently stolen by a heron and I would shout at him if I saw him coming in to land.

As a teenager taking the short (and banned) cut across a park to school I had two options. I cycled past the No Cycling signs and therefore was chased and reported by the brown clad park-keeper or I walked with my bike and met the wrath of the Canada geese protecting their young. I usually decided that the park-keeper was the lesser of the two evils because I could cycle faster than he could run and anyway I was also late for school and couldn't waste time walking. It left me with a long time aversion to Canada geese but since I've been on the rivers I have been able to observe them at closer quarters. I have found it fascinating to watch how they work as a community to guard their young. During the day they are mainly grazing in the fields, in the evening they come down to the river for their constitutional swim and to drink and preen. They form groups according to the age of the chicks. A group of three families with three week old chicks, two families with six week goslings, four families with gangly teenagers. The parents are at the front and rear and patrolling the boundaries and the young stay in a line in the middle. As the night approaches they go back to the fields and the young huddle together and the adults form a barrier around them. Canada geese lay up to seven eggs, if you count the young in each family they often number seven. The death rate seems low, perhaps the feckless mallards should take note of the parenting regime of the Canada geese and they too may have a higher survival rate amongst their chicks.

I was moored on the Great Ouse a few miles south of Ely and a family of Canada geese came onto the river. They swam along the water in a straight line with father in the lead, followed by three of his young, then one Greylag goose of the same size and age as the Canada youngsters, three more of his own youngsters then mother bringing up the rear. A few days later, in Ely I saw a family of Greylags which consisted of five of their own young and one young Canada goose. Had they decided to swap babies? Hasn't anybody noticed that one of their children is a bit different to the rest? Will the misplaced off-spring have an identity crisis in later life and need counselling?

I was feeding bread to a group of Canada geese and their goslings when a pair of swans joined in. A gosling nipped in front of the cob to reach a bit of bread, the swan promptly grabbed it by the neck, dunked it under the water and held it there. By the time I found a weapon to attack the swan the body of the gosling was floating downstream.

I do not know why Danny Kaye sang about the ugly duckling that turned into a swan. Cygnets are beautiful. They are pale grey bundles of fluff, trying to stretch fledgling wings, scurrying after their mothers, peep peeping for food from adoring spectators. On the riverbank at Ely a swan came floating along, her wings were curved outwards and on her back sat four little grey cygnets, safe and secure and enjoying the ride. The aaaah factor was high. The cameras came out. She glided over towards proffered bread, the cameras clicked, a Canada goose came over to join in so the mother swan promptly attacked him and in the process unceremoniously dumped her babies in the river. I blame the mothers for the aggression of swans.

Bottisham Lock

'We went on a boating holiday once before on that Midi Canal in France. The first afternoon we came across a body, a young bloke that had committed suicide, well I don't know what his problems were but he didn't get our holiday off to a good start, I can tell you. Then we were stuck for a week on this straight boring canal, couldn't see over the banks just long rows of trees reflecting in the mucky, oily water and there was coypu everywhere, big rat things glaring out of the undergrowth at us, horrible they were. We had bikes with us, we thought we'd cycle to the villages, have a glass of wine in a bar but every time we got to a village it was closed.'

This holiday isn't going too well either. The lady on the hired river cruiser is telling her tale of woe to four of us standing on the lock-side. She is below us in the empty, murky depths of the lock trapped there, on the boat, because the mechanism of the lock is jammed and the gate will neither open nor allow water to be let back in.

I'd set off from Cambridge just before lunch-time planning to get to Ely by early evening but I haven't got far, only about six miles downriver and through the first lock and now I'm held up at the second.

'I've got arthritis in my knees so I can't climb the ladder to get out,' she continues her monologue. 'They're not easy to get out of, these boats, I've hardly been out of this one all week. Derek's got to do it all, drive, do the locks, moor up. He shouldn't be doing all

141

that pushing and pulling and climbing around, not with his heart. Mr Radcliffe said to him, "Derek you've got to start taking it easy," but he doesn't take any notice. We had a nasty time when we were mooring up the other night and Derek was on the bank and couldn't hold the boat because of the wind. He had to yell instructions at me so I could move the boat. I thought we were both going to have a heart attack that time.'

I wonder why, if she can't get in and out, she hasn't learned to steer the boat but frequently women on boats don't have a clue how to handle them. I'm never sure if it's fear on the women's part or it's because their men folk take charge and never give them the chance to learn to do supposedly difficult manly things like steering boats. I think maybe the latter; driving a boat is a lot less physically demanding than working the locks and more interesting than polishing the brass work.

However, she hasn't been wasting her time whilst she's been stuck on the boat with only the dank and slimy lock walls to look at. She's baked a Victoria sponge and the sweet cakey smell is drifting upwards.

'It's not as light as I usually get it. This PLJ gas isn't very good for sponge cakes.'

The Environment Agency have been called and a man is coming down to see if he can get the lock gate open, he'll be here when he's finished having tea with his auntie in Argyll. There's a broken down cruiser tied-up at the lock mooring and the repair man will be coming to that, when he's finished having tea with his auntie in Taunton. I tried to hover in the river but the wind had other ideas so the tip of my bow is on the lock mooring and the rest of the boat is embedded in banks of rosebay willow herb and purple loosestrife.

Occasionally people hove into view along the flood bank, ask what the hold-up is and go back to report to other boaters waiting upriver. On the other side of the lock, tempers aren't being improved by two narrow boats, heading downstream, but first stopped at the lock moorings for a boozy picnic; they are causing difficulties to the increasing number of boats that are coming upstream and want to moor up to go through the lock.

But it's a warm, breezy, sunny day and all us stranded here are whiling away the afternoon, enjoying not being able to go anywhere. Slices of warm cake have been handed up and chat has divided along gender lines, the women are discussing baking (although my input is minimal as I am better at eating cakes than baking them) and the men, along with two passing dog walkers from the nearby houses, are talking about gearboxes. Six soldiers, fully laden, stomp, stomp, stomp across the metal bridge their faces red and perspiration pouring off them. 'Almost home lads,' shouts one of the dog walkers. The back marker raises a weary hand. Waterbeach barracks, their assumed destination, is a mile away across the fields.

From the downstream side a man steams in, his white hair and beard contrasting with his red face. He's fuming at people who picnic at lock moorings and idiots who can't operate locks properly. He demands to know how we caused the problem and what we've done to try and remedy it. He stalks over to the box with all the buttons and levers in, jabs the Raise Gate button and the allegedly jammed gate starts moving slowly upwards.

So that's all we needed, a red faced, bad tempered man with a beard to sort us out.

We say our goodbyes and drift off back to our boats. The trapped boat and its cake-maker are released and I start to plan how to exit from my flower bed with the broken down cruiser at a sharp angle in front of me and a strong side breeze holding me on the bank. I decide to reverse off the bank into the centre of the river and then turn into the lock, so push my rear end out of the vegetation with the pole. My new acquaintances decide to be helpful and push my front end out with their boat hook. The law of physics dictates that on a long solid boat if the front end is pushed out the back end will come back in. So as my front end goes out my back end comes back in, the wind catches me and I am back where I started from: stranded in the weeds. I wave my hand to indicate, 'Don't bother pushing.' They all stand on the bank gaily waving back. I push my back end out, they push my front end out, my back end comes back in. I try to signal, 'No' with both hands; they all wave back even more enthusiastically.

After the fourth time of push back end out, watch the helpers push front end out, watch back end come back in, wave to the helpers, watch the helpers wave back I am resigned to the fact that I'm not going to complete my exit from the bank in the manner in which I had planned it. I think, 'Oh bugger it' and manoeuvre out as best I can, narrowly missing the broken down cruiser and scraping the lock-side as I drive in. Then as the problematic gate grinds down I do a proper farewell wave and all my helpers wave back.

I'd planned to be in Ely by early evening but it is already early evening and I have another three hours of journey ahead of me. The drunken lock-side picnickers decide to move on just as I'm about to come out of the lock and they are ahead of me slowly weaving their way in tandem along the river, music blaring from loud speakers. I overtake them and gradually leave them behind and their music slowly fades away into the pale evening light.

The stretch of the river from Bottisham Lock to Ely is alive with birds and waterfowl. At the Five Mile from Anywhere pub, a marsh harrier rises from the fields. Moorhens and coots scuttle at the water's edge. Cormorants, grebes and terns dive for fish. There are droves of swans a-swimming, mainly unattached juveniles looking as if they're out for the Saturday evening with their mates.

Ahead of me six swans take flight and fly low towards the boat. It appears we are on collision course but they rise at the last minute to clear the bow, the whup, whup, whup of their wings sounds above the noise of the engine as they pass low overhead.

The banks are knee deep in herons, there are so many of them I wonder if there is a heronry in the nearby wood. I'm not sure what a heronry looks like, I suspect it's a lot of large nests but I can't see any large nests in the trees. I'm told that you can locate a heronry by the smell, I sniff the air but all I can smell is the diesel from my engine.

A pair of Egyptian geese glide past peering up at me through kohl rimmed eyes they are followed by a posse of indeterminate ducks that all appear to be a variation on the theme of mallard.

A pair of Oyster Catchers ferret on the mud banks, a little egret takes flight, bright white against the darkening fields. An almost as white barn owl flies alongside before turning and diving over the river behind my stern where I'd seen a mallard and her four chicks foraging in the weeds along the bank.

There's a skirmish going on in the river ahead of me. I can't see it properly but it looks like one of those nasty swans attacking a moorhen. When I get closer I see it's a moorhen attacking a swan. The swan is only a youngster, by the flecks of beige amongst his feathers I can tell that he's one of last year's brood so maybe he hasn't developed the territorial aggression of a full grown male. He isn't putting up a fight against his bantam weight opponent, he's in retreat. The moorhen follows, flying at him and pecking at his neck. Further on another moorhen has four chicks following maybe these are the attacking moorhen's family and the reason for his aggression. The chicks are little black scraps of fluff peep peeping shrilly as they progress. One is a bit of a laggard, suddenly there is a splash and flash of silver and large increasing circles in the water and now the moorhen has only three chicks. It's a precarious existence on the river when you're a scrap of fluff at the bottom of the food chain.

It's dusk when I reach Ely and manage to just

squeeze into what seems to be the last mooring space. It's dark when half an hour later the party picnickers pass by, the music still thumping.

Ten minutes later I hear the beat of their music heading back down the river, 'You overtook us so you could get the last mooring space,' they call out cheerily.

'Of course I did. If you can't find anywhere you can moor up alongside me.' I offer magnanimously, hoping that they don't want to moor alongside me. Luckily their boats are a bit shorter than mine and they manage to find a gap to fit into and moor side by side outside The Cutter pub where they can join in with and provide music for the Saturday night drinkers who are spilling across the pavement.

Can't Be Too Careful

'G.J. Reeves' hull,' says my newly arrived neighbour, nodding in the direction of my boat.

'Yes,' I say. He has that look in his eye. A, 'Go on ask me how I know, ask me how I know, go on, ask me,' look.

So I don't ask him how he knows the hull of my boat was made by G.J. Reeves. I've just spent over an hour in conversation with one of the anoraks of the waterways. I have no intention of being trapped by another one. To say I was in conversation with the anorak is stretching the point; he was talking, I was listening, or half listening or, after the first ten minutes, not listening at all. He was giving me more information than I could ever need to know about batteries and wattage and amps and connectors and inverters and alternators. And his flies were undone.

I know that my new neighbour's comments about the G.J Reeves hull are no more than his opening conversational gambit. As soon as I show a slightest interest in how he knows the hull was manufactured by G.J Reeves his next move will be to tell me everything I already know about the entire specification of my boat. Then he'll want to know what gearbox I've got, and tell me that I would be better using something with an unpronounceable name that is only available if you visit their factory in the Outer Hebrides. He'll do a lengthy discourse on engines and water pumps and solar panels and he'll never once pause for breath. He'll inform me about which oil to use and oil filters and air filters and where to get the cheapest and best. Not once, not once during the never ending spiel will he look at me and think, 'Those aren't the fingernails of a woman who services her own engine,' or even notice that I've fallen asleep and I'm curled up at his feet snoring loudly.

Oh no, I'm not giving him the chance to start a conversation. My, 'Yes,' is curt and I bury my head in the book I'm trying to read hoping he'll take the hint and go away.

He looks crestfallen at my lack of interest in his encyclopaedic knowledge of manufacturers of boats and goes back to adjusting his mooring ropes. He gets out two chains and padlocks his boat to the bollards. Now he's got my interest, 'I've never seen that done before,' I tell him.

'Can't be too careful,' he says, 'I've been cast adrift here in Ely before now. Drunken tykes coming out of the pub think it's funny to untie boats. I woke up and found myself heading off downriver, got it back under control before I got to the railway bridge but they let Lady Blatherwick loose as well, there was nobody on board and she carried on until her bows got stuck in that soft bank at Queen Adelaide.' That sounds like the plot of a Victorian melodrama.

A rotund Rottweiler gets off his boat, defecates and then wanders over towards me. I look at it warily.

'She won't harm you,' he says 'she's as gentle as a kitten.' I think of the kittens I've known who could decimate a pair of curtains in minutes and tear a friendly hand to shreds in seconds and they were only a fraction of the size of this dog. I hope he's a lot gentler than a kitten or I'm in trouble.

The rotund Rottweiler is followed off the boat by two rotund Jack Russell terriers who duly defecate on the same bit of grass. Now if they were the size of the Rottweiler I would be even more worried. I do not trust Jack Russells, nasty vicious little beasts almost as bad as the swans. Judging by the pot bellies on the three four-legged inhabitants of Morning Breeze they aren't taken for many long country walks. Their equally portly owner does not seem capable of leaning over his own pot belly and picking up the excrement.

'You can't be too careful,' he says and points at the dogs. 'Nobody's going to mess with me when there's a Rottweiler and those two on board. I was up Denver way and some Latvians had a line across the river, it's totally illegal fishing like that, so I cut the line. Anyway they didn't like that, came chasing down the river bank after me to where I was mooring up. They were looking to cause trouble. Just called the dogs and they stood next to me. Those Latvians took one look at the Rottweiler and didn't come a step nearer. Did a bit of shouting and fist waving then they went on their way. They had more sense than to mess with her. You should get a big dog, lots of problems around here with all these Eastern Europeans on the farms and packing stations. Always putting out illegal nets and lines, they catch the fish to eat them, that's wrong they shouldn't be eating the fish they should return them to the river.'

I think that catching fish to eat is a lot more sensible than catching fish to weigh and throw back but don't want to argue with a fat man, a Rottweiler and two Jack Russell terriers.

I don't feel the need for protective dogs because if I did come across illegal fishing lines I wouldn't cut them, I'd just ignore them and sail on by thereby avoiding dinner deprived Latvians chasing me along the riverbank.

'Lots of funny people around here.' He said, 'I've got a revolver, not loaded, of course, but if I sit there and point it at an intruder they don't know it isn't loaded and they're going to get off my boat pretty sharpish. Got a catapult as well, that's loaded with ball bearings and I know how to use that. Nobody is going to come aboard Morning Mist uninvited.'

Ely seems a peaceful sort of place and the need for a complete armoury seems unnecessary. Although I could be wrong maybe the descendants of Hereward the Wake still live around here and maybe their aggressive ancestral blood awakens and stirs them into perceiving all boaters as river borne invaders and launching attacks on them. At which point Morning Mist's dogs, guns and catapults will come in very useful and maybe the addition of a few vats of boiling oil and a machine that pelts rocks would help as well.

The sun had gone in and there was a sudden chill to the air. I packed up my chair and book and moved them inside. Then I went and adjusted the mooring ropes tying the knots on the far side of the boat. That way if any inebriated reveller was leaving the pubs at closing time and thinking it would be fun to set me afloat they would have to climb on board to reach over and untie the ropes.

My theory is that would cause the boat to rock, it would wake me up and I would spring out of bed, immediately adopt the position of deadly Kung-Fu fighter, screech in a fearful manner and all marauders would be so frightened they'd run off into the night. Reality might not fit the theory because there are two major flaws to the theory. The first flaw is that I sleep the sleep of the dead and a bit of gentle rocking is likely to send me into a deeper sleep rather than startle me into a wakefulness that was ready to repel all boarders. Secondly, I am a coward and if I did actually wake up to find strangers on my boat I'd just dive under the duvet, feign sleep and wait until they'd stolen all my belongings, set the boat free and I was floating down towards the North Sea.

After I'd adjusted the ropes I locked and bolted the doors and hatches and checked the windows. After all you can't be too careful.

The sky had darkened and the air had stilled, dense black clouds advanced across the distant fields trailing their tattered grey skirts of rain. Without the sun to illuminate it and the wind to mottle it the river calmed to smooth, burnished pewter. Only minutes earlier the shoals of roach which had gathered around the hull had been brightly visible, the light of the sun penetrating the water had highlighted the orange tips of their fins. Now they had once more become invisible in the darkened depths of their own private world, the only sign of their continuing presence was brief flashes of silver followed by the ripples of concentric circles that widened, flattened and faded.

More noticeable were the sluggish splashes of a large fish which turned and churned and muddied the deeper water under the dense weeds on the far bank. Every so often its dull grey back squirmed above the surface. According to one of the bankside anglers it is probably a large carp, one that had spent its long lifetime here, frequently hooked and hauled out of the river, weighed, measured, photographed and then thrown back in. I hope it hadn't become too complacent and become used to making the most of the tempting morsels on the ends of fishing lines secure in the knowledge that the tasty meal might involve a bit of inconvenience but all would be well in the end. The Latvians and Eastern Europeans who are employed in the vegetable packing station a few miles along the bank haven't grasped the concept of catch, weigh, measure, throw back. They just catch, cook and eat. If they catch this old-timer he'll provide a good dinner.

Near to where the carp squirms, the cows and calves have come down to the river to drink and are kneeling precariously on the bank, noses in the river. I can hear them drawing in the water, making a noise like a child with a straw reaching the end of its strawberry milk-shake. Above them a barn owl quarters the water meadow, searching for prey, I focus my binoculars on it and can see clearly its sharp black eyes in the beautiful, flat, white face.

The announcements, from the railway station behind

the marina, usually an incoherent babble of disembodied voices, can be heard clearly in the stillness of this evening. 'The train on Platform One is the 8.45 for King's Lynn'. Minutes later the First Capital Connect train to King's Lynn gathers speed as it clatters over the rail bridge ahead. In its wake is an endless goods train. The black engine drags its load, a line of aggregate wagons labelled Maersk, Maersk, Maersk, Maersk, a dozen empty trailers, containers, more aggregate wagons Lafarge, Lafarge, Lafarge Lafarge, glass wagons, empty platforms all relentlessly thud, thud, thudding over the bridge.

The encroaching clouds bring a premature end to the day. The willow tree on the opposite bank no longer casts its reflection onto the river, now it only forms a filigree of a silhouette against the orange glow of the lights of Stuntney, the village beyond the water meadows.

I think that Stuntney is an onomatopoeia of a name for a Fenland village. In his poem Granchester Rupert Brooke says Cambridge people are, 'Urban, squat and full of guile,' he could have extended that description to most of the natives of the Fens. The Fen villages share the physical characteristics of the inhabitants, although mostly they lack the guile. I imagine Stuntney consists of a squat church, a few stolid Georgian houses and Victorian farm workers houses and a line of low bungalows all with their foundations gradually sinking into the black peat of the fen. If I am wrong and it is a picture postcard village with thatched roofs, duck ponds and village greens I will readily extend my apologies to Stuntney.

In the early hours of the morning I am woken by the rocking of the boat and by banging and bumping. For a few panicky minutes I think that I am being invaded by the drunken hordes of Ely and I'm about to be cast adrift upon the waters of the Great Ouse. Then I realise that a storm has blown up. The wind is howling and the strength of it is beating the boat against the wooden pontoon. Heavy rain is drumming on the roof and windows.

It's too noisy to sleep so I get up to make a cup of coffee and switch on the World Service to keep me company and to try and blot out the disturbing noises. The boat is being buffeted by the gale force wind, the river has been whipped into turbulent life and it feels as if I'm at sea instead of on a normally placid inland river. Motion sickness is imminent. I can hear the groan of the ropes as they take the strain of the boat pushing and pulling against the mooring posts. It is unsettling to wake in the early hours of the morning and find your home being shaken violently and to hear water thrashing about only inches from your feet. The vulnerability of a boat is highlighted in a storm. In gale force winds a house may feel shaken and lose tiles or even the roof but they rarely sink and they never break free of their moorings and get carried off downriver.

I must have fallen asleep despite the rattling, banging and rocking and the howling of the wind because when I wake there is a grey, watery daylight peering in from behind the blinds. It's a windy, squally day, pulses of rain drum across the roof and the boat is still in motion. The usually placid Great Ouse has been transformed into a frothing, fast flowing, khaki stretch of water. The high wind is whipping the surface of the river into wavelets. Bits of dead reeds, twigs, weeds and branches move rapidly past my window. Three wind and tide assisted mallards zoom downstream, giving a quick hopeful look over their shoulders, but they have passed on by before they can discern if the woman at the window is holding bread. All the other river dwellers have taken cover. The usual squawks of ducks, honks of geese and cries of terns and gulls are absent. The herd of cows and calves has taken shelter under the far-off trees. There are no House Martins swooping for insects. The sound of the station announcements have been blanketed by the roar of the wind. The road is devoid of cars. The world contrives to be both stormily noisy and eerily quiet.

The only creatures that are enjoying the weather are Ely's platoon of ugly Muscovy ducks; they have left the river and are happily splashing in and drinking from the puddles that have formed on the quayside. I wonder why when they have a large river flowing past that they find muddy puddles so enticing and so much fun.

On a Sunday morning, at this time of the year the river would be busy with rowers, canoes, cruisers and narrow boats. The little brown cruise boat would be taking tourists on trips along the river, the guide on the back giving a commentary, his black Labrador curled up at his feet. But like the wildlife, the boaters and the tourists have stayed away, the river is empty, the riverside pathway is empty, the fields are empty and the only inhabitants of the skies are the scurrying grey clouds.

The one exception is a hired river cruiser which is probably due to be returned to Bridge Boatyards that morning. It comes past my kitchen window at full throttle, he obviously needs the power to counteract the effect of the wind, but this combined with the fast current means that he is travelling at the speed of sound and surfers could follow on his wash. The turn into Bridge Boatyards marina is tight and he is travelling too fast to manage that turn easily. Shouted instructions and curses carry on the wind.

Despite all the shouted advice he must have missed the entrance because a few minutes later he comes past again, this time moving sideways along the river. The driver is wrestling with the wheel, a woman is standing at the bow holding a rope and in the cabin two little boys, togged up in yellow life-jackets peer, pale faced and wide-eyed, out of the window.

The driver tries to turn the boat, the wind thinks it's a game and joins in sending him pirouetting towards the stanchions of the road bridge. Another Bridge Boatyards boat, complete with crew, ropes and grappling hooks, comes alongside him. Maybe the intention is to help but from my vantage point it looks as if the second boat has just come to his companion in a waltz along the river. They dance around each other for a few minutes then tango back in a crablike motion, engines revving, exhaust fumes billowing in the wind. There's a lot of shouting between the crews but not a lot of action. I, and a few others, leave the calm of our boats and stand on our bows, braced against the elements offering to catch ropes, yelling unhelpful advice and in general being as much use as chocolate teapots.

The boats make hard fought progress along the river then they suddenly disappear from view. The shouting ceases abruptly so I assume they have managed to reach the comparative calm of the marina.

Either that or they've sunk and all on board are drowned.

Safety

Maybe I should be a bit more concerned about my safety although I don't think I could ever take the extreme measures of Fat Steve on Morning Mist and share a boat with three dogs, a cross-bow, a revolver (unloaded of course) and a collection of padlocks. If I was that concerned about marauders I wouldn't live on a boat, I'd go and live in a castle.

I've frequently been advised to get a dog for protection but I'm not really a dog person. I prefer cats and a fat lot of good a cat would be at protecting me from potential assailants. When I toyed with the idea of getting a dog I thought about getting a greyhound. There's many a failed greyhound that needs re-housing. Greyhounds don't have a lot of hair to shed so I wouldn't have to hoover too often, or more likely in my case I wouldn't have to wade through even more dust and fluff than I have to now. They don't need a lot of exercise, one brief bout of speed a day will do and as a bonus they might bring home the occasional hare. Then somebody tells me greyhounds fart a lot so I decide that I'm not getting a greyhound. There's enough strange smells on this boat without a farting dog adding to them.

The main advantage of using a dog as a security measure is that they bark. Someone tries to break in, the dog barks ferociously, the someone expects to be mauled by a vicious dog and goes away. Therefore I don't need a dog I just need a bark. Somebody must have produced a bark as a type of burglar alarm so I look on the internet and sure enough there are several. I decide I will just get a bark, it doesn't need feeding or grooming, there are no vets bills just a bit of wiring and I will have all the security of apparently owning a large dog without having to take it for a walk or feed it. Then I wonder if an electronic bark will be heavy on the batteries and I realise I can't order it over the internet because I don't have an address where goods can be sent and with my electrical abilities I'd probably fuse everything on the boat when I tried to wire it in. So in the end I don't get either a dog or a bark.

One of the things that made me buy Rea (apart from the damage she inflicted on my ex-husband) was the fact I felt safe on her. When I went into the bedroom and switched on the down lighters and closed the door I felt cocooned and safe. That feeling has never left. I still feel safe when I am on board.

It did take a while to get used to unfamiliar and sometimes worrying sounds. When you live in a house the noises both internal and external are part of your everyday existence, you know the sound of central heating switching off, the creak of the floorboards, of the wind rapping that branch of honeysuckle against the window. You know the sounds of traffic, of the neighbours, of the dogs and the night-time calls of foxes. You know when the gate clicks in the early hours of the morning it is the milkman. When a car starts at 5am it is just Jim next door going to work. When you hear voices late at night it is just the teenagers across the road coming home from a party. On a boat that is moored in a different place every other night the outside noises are always unfamiliar. Is it normal for somebody to cycle past the window at midnight or run along the towpath in the early hours of the morning? Is that shouting only people leaving a pub or is there a riot happening nearby? Why's that dog barking? What's that scrabbling about outside?

I quickly got used to the noises of the boat. The strange crackling noise along the roof sounded as if somebody was running across it but was only the roof croaking as the temperature dropped and the metal contracted. The funny bumping noise along the side of the boat was swans and ducks chabbling at the weed that had adhered to the hull. I identified the annoying drone of the fridge, the sound of the water pump switching itself on and the bleep bleep of the inverter switching itself off. It was the external noises that varied, sometimes it was the rumble of traffic if I was near a road, or of trains if I was near a rail track, or of drunks if I was near a pub. In urban areas there was distant music and the screech of police sirens. In a rural area it was the noise of combine harvesters working through the night and the screech of owls or of coots. I'd work out that the bleeping noise wasn't something going wrong with the electrical system just the sound of a distant automatic level crossing and that the early morning voices outside my waterside window weren't waterborne assailants just early risers from the downriver rowing club. Then the next day I'd move on and the noises outside would be different and I'd have to adapt to a whole new set of sounds.

I also lost my sense of time. I used to have a good idea of the time by the light and the external noises. The resident blackbird starting his pre-dawn warm-up meant I had a few more hours in bed. The hiss of the air-brakes as the first bus braked to go round the bend meant rising was imminent. The sound of children on their way to school meant I'd overslept again and was going to be late for work. When the sun reached the side window it was 2pm when the noise of the traffic increased it was time to open the bottle of wine. Now I had no points of reference, even dawn was variable depending on whether I was moored amongst open fields or under trees. Did it seem light because the sun was rising or was I near strong street lamps? I had hoped to live a life where I got up when I wanted to and wasn't governed by clocks but the reality was different and I still have to work and trains didn't run on a, 'When Stephanie is ready to get up,' timetable. I had to resort to putting batteries in the kitchen clock and making sure my mobile phone showed more or less the right time but I've never got desperate enough to know the time that I've had to buy a watch.

I did find that when you live in the same place an unexpected and unfamiliar noise can startle you awake and keep you awake as your ears strain to hear it and identify it. Yet when I was mooring in different places, sometimes rural and isolated sometimes urban and busy, all noises were strange and unfamiliar so I learned to ignore them all and sleep soundly.

The only place I was concerned about a strange

sound and a loud bang was when I was moored in Peterborough. I was warned that the quayside in Peterborough was a bit of a dodgy place to moor. It was late evening and dark and I was reading when the boat suddenly rocked violently. It felt as if somebody had climbed on board. I sat stock still, heart pounding, and waited to see what would happen. Nothing happened. The boat stabilised. I peered out from behind the curtain and strained my eyes to see across the park, there were a few youths gathered around a distant bench but otherwise it was deserted. On the river side of the boat all was quiet. My pounding heart gradually returned to normal and I calmed down and went to bed but I seemed to stay on high alert for quite a time. In the morning when I went out I found that a narrowboat was moored up behind me his bow tightly against my stern. He must have arrived after dark and bumped and banged his way into a tight space. If I'd had the courage to open the door and look out I would have realised what had happened and saved myself some worry, although I still wouldn't have slept properly the screeching from the factory opposite would have seen to that.

I hear many stories about crime and vandalism on the waterways. There are the boater's tales of theft, bricks thrown from bridges, ripped cratch covers and broken windows. Ware in Hertfordshire seemed to feature heavily in the tales of mishaps. Three times I heard of a knife attack on a cratch cover and the boat broken into and possessions stolen. I'm not sure whether I heard three stories of the same incident or there were three separate incidents because each time the details of the attack and the items stolen differed marginally. It may be that the changes and embellishments had occurred in the telling and instead of a worrying wave of boat crime in Ware there had only ever been one small event. Even so I have been warned to stay away from Ware. It is a hotbed of crime. I'm told that the Eastern Europeans are the ones responsible for all the theft and only last week police stopped a group of Latvians progressing along the High Street with two dead swans strapped to their backs. Those pesky Latvians they'll eat anything.

When I was stopped at a lock near Wellingborough I was given dire warnings by a farmer.

'Watch out when you come into Wellingborough, those erks jump from bridges onto the roof then run into the cabin and nick anything they can then when they get to the next bridge their mates haul them and the loot up. Lock your doors and keep to the middle of the river and don't stop.' He told me.

As usual I ignored the good advice. I stopped for the night in Wellingborough and I didn't have any problems. In his book, Waterworld, Richard Deakin had told of similar experiences reported in Well Creek where it runs through Upwell and Outwell. I didn't experience any problems in either place.

I read in a boating magazine about bricks being dropped on boaters passing under bridges in Wigan and I heard of boats being untied and left adrift in Wolverhampton. Latvians in Ware, theft in Wellingborough, bricks in Wigan, idiots in

Wolverhampton, bridge jumpers in Well Creek. The only common factor I can see is that most trouble appears to happen in places beginning with W so in the interests of safety I'll try and stay away from all places where the names begin with W.

The other bit of advice given by the bankside harbingers of doom is, 'Don't go to Bedford'. This isn't because of the high crime rate of Bedford it's because of the owners of river cruisers. People on river cruisers don't like narrow boats and it would appear that the boaters of Bedford are a particularly belligerent lot. As far as I am aware the boaters of Bedford aren't in the habit of causing damage to narrow boats, they just refuse to talk to their inhabitants and moor leaving spaces that another cruiser could get into but isn't long enough for a full length narrow boat. According to the legends of the river the plan to link the canal system to Bedford (the last navigable point on the Great Ouse) is opposed by the boaters in Bedford because they are sure it would bring more narrow boats onto their stretch of river. It would. At the moment it takes about three weeks on a meandering route to get from the canal system to Bedford. If the link, from Bedford to a point near Milton Keynes on the Grand Union Canal, was completed it would take two or three days at the most and make a circular route possible. Narrow boaters like nothing better than not having to go back the way they came and they would come flooding through. I don't think the river cruiser owners of Bedford should lose too much sleep over this nightmare scenario because I can't see that the link is likely to be started, let alone finished, within their lifetimes, especially given that most cruiser owners seem elderly and haven't got a lot of life-time left.

I can see why the river cruisers don't like narrow boats. Narrow boats are long and take up a lot of room at mooring points, they move slowly and can block a curvy river for an age before the faster travelling cruiser can overtake. Also one good thump from a hefty steel narrow boat could completely demolish a fibreglass cruiser. Narrow boats are built for canals and river cruisers are built for rivers and ocean going yachts are built for the ocean and if all stayed in their respective places then there would be no need for all this animosity. My narrow boat should really be on the canals but I have decided I prefer rivers; they are much more interesting with more wildlife and more variety and water that moves instead of just sitting murkily still and shallow. The river cruisers will just have to put up with me.

I'm not sure what the narrow boat dwellers have against the cruisers apart from the fact that driven fast they do produce a lot of wash. Narrow boat owners are very disparaging about the cruisers calling them The Plastics and Tupperware and Yoghurt Pots or the most derogatory term Plastic Pigs. I don't like going into locks or mooring in tight spaces amongst river cruisers but that is because of a lack of confidence in my ability to steer safely. A few wrong moves or a strong side wind make me fear collisions, squashed boats and bloodied bodies all followed by acrimonious and expensive insurance claims.

I have observed that when a group of boats are moored together the cruiser owners talk to the other cruiser owners and the narrow boat owners talk to other narrow boat owners and couples talk to couples and lone boaters talk to lone boaters. The live-aboards are referred to as water gypsies. I rather like being called a water gypsy. I have visions of myself in lots of flowing skirts (a bit of hazard in locks) and beads and earrings and a new found ability to dance and play the tambourine. But I don't think when we are referred to as water gypsies we are perceived as colourful characters living a romantic way of life. We are just perceived as down and outs in need of a good wash.

Hanging Around

Maybe I'm not a true born again boater because I find the best bit of boating is the stopping. Cruising along the waterways is fine but after the first couple of hours, unless there is something really interesting to see, I get a bit fed up of moving so slowly and my legs start to ache from standing at the helm, I need a coffee and I need a pee and invariably it starts to rain. If I see something of interest on the bank I want to walk over and see it.

On the canals it is fine, easy to stop and go and explore a bit of countryside or a village. Here on the Great Ouse it is more difficult because the stopping places can be long distances apart and when I get there they are often full. The other problem is that mooring at almost all the mooring sites is limited to forty eight hours. In Ely and Cambridge the local councils have riparian rights along the riverbank and they send out the bankside equivalent of traffic wardens to take names and numbers and slap notices threatening prosecution for those that have overstayed their welcome. The rest of the moorings are either GOBA (Great Ouse Boating Association) moorings which are often rough moorings in isolated places or Environment Agency Moorings. The Environment Agency don't have the resources or manpower to continually check the length of time boats have been moored, especially as some of the moorings are remote so they only clamp down when they notice, or are told by other boaters, that somebody is really flaunting the rules.

I still need to work, all plans to quit work and float around the waterways system came to an abrupt halt with the arrival of the first bank statement after I'd moved onto the boat. I am also buying a flat in London in conjunction with my daughter and the paperwork is slow and the negotiations tortuous and I have decided to be in an area of good communications until it is all sorted out then I will go back to my original plan of moving onto the canals. I have a good internet connection here, my dongle works at full strength and I can get to London easily which is where most of my work is. The rail connections from Cambridge and Huntingdon are good but better from Ely and Waterbeach where the railway station is more accessible from the river. So for a few weeks I will pootle along from Cambridge to Ely and stop at all points between. Good reasons all for not moving towards the canal system and becoming a lone female boater continuously cruising along the waterways.

Maybe I'm just looking for excuses to stick around an area I know near to friends, family and familiarity.

This week I have a small problem in that I need to be around Ely for over a week: a day's work on Monday: hang around for a few days: another day's work on Thursday. I'm not allowed to stay in Ely for more than forty eight hours and the river traffic warden walking past my boat every morning at 8.30 notes the boat name and registration number so they know exactly how long I have been there. I decide on Tuesday and Wednesday I will go four miles upriver and stay at the quiet mooring at Little Thetford and then come back again, thereby not overstaying my allocated time in Ely and not having a brown envelope pushed under my cratch cover threatening legal action and fines of a thousand pounds.

It is very quiet at Little Thetford, it's far from any roads there is only the intermittent calls of the waterfowl, lowing of cattle and the hum of passing trains from the tracks beyond the high flood bank. I'm the only boat moored there on the Tuesday evening. I sit in the bow of the boat armed with a book I'm not reading and a bottle of red wine that I am drinking, a blanket around my legs in case the evening gets chilly. This is the part of living on a boat that I've come to love, this is the part that makes enduring all the other inconveniences worthwhile. To just sit in the bow, alone on my boat watching the day fade and seeing the changing of light across the wide river is magical. The wind dies away and the waterfowl quieten, there is a distant call of an owl. The water flattens and the setting sun is reflected on the surface and then slowly it changes with a multitude of differing colours and reflections as darkness falls. Then stars gradually appear in the blackening sky. I sit and watch faint glimmers of light across the water. The quietness of the night is only broken by the rumble of the trains that pass by every half hour.

It is after 10am on this dark moonless night when I hear somebody calling, 'Hello' 'Excuse Me. Hello. Hello.' I look out at the opposite bank, I can see the glow of a torch. I stand up in the bow.

'Hello,' I call back.

'Excuse me, you know which is the way to Barway?' a young woman's voice asks in halting English.

I think for a few minutes. Looking out I can see the lights of a habitation on the other side of the bank.

'I come from Ely, I live Barway but maybe I don't find path in dark.'

I remember seeing a public footpath leading off the flood bank down towards Barway.

'Yes,' I shout back. 'You are in the right direction the path is about another ten minutes on the left over a stile.'

'You sure?' she asks doubtfully.

'Yes, I'm sure.'

The beam of the torch moves off and I go back in the boat. It takes a few minutes for it to dawn on me that it is likely that she wants to get to the vegetable packing plant at Barway where there is accommodation for the seasonal foreign workers. That is a couple of miles north of the village of Barway and the pathway is beside a pumping station about a mile back the way she had come. By the time I have found my torch and my shoes and have climbed the steps onto the flood bank at this side of the river to tell her she is heading in the wrong direction she has disappeared, I can't see the beam of a torch in either direction.

I worry about her for a few days but I presume she got back safely, she sounded young and fit and it was a mild night and I never did see any reports of missing Eastern European girls or of bodies found in the river.

The following morning a young man tapped on my roof.

'Had I seen a calf stuck in the mud?' he asked. I hadn't but I had heard a lot of lowing from the cattle on the bank about half an hour ago.

'Which direction did the noise come from?' I'd just sent the last person that asked for a location in completely the wrong direction so I was a bit wary when I said, 'Upriver on the opposite bank. Maybe.'

The young man was from the fire brigade. They had been notified by the police who had been notified by a passing boater that a calf was stuck in the mud at the edge of the river. There were a few firemen scattered along the bank and I joined them to look for the stranded calf. And my sole purpose in joining them was to help a distressed animal; it wasn't so I could wander around the countryside with some fit young men. Honest. Our search for the calf was to no avail. Maybe it had dropped into the same black hole as my missing walker.

I was surprised that it was the responsibility of the fire brigade and not the responsibility of the farmer to retrieve the calf but I suppose if the fire brigade rescue cats from trees there is no reason why they shouldn't rescue calves from mud.

While I'm here I'm reading a book about Hereward the Wake by Peter Rex. The writer suggests that the Normans landed at this spot in about 1071 after two unsuccessful attempts to reach Ely across Aldreth Causeway. It is rumoured that a monk betrayed Hereward and his force, he told the Normans of a safe path across marshland. The Norman forces were able to reach the monastery at Ely and crush the rebellion against them. There are many stories of Hereward, some are fact and many are fiction. It is documented that he led the fight against the Normans and that he was fighting from the Isle of Ely. A thousand years ago, before the major drainage of the Fens that took place in the seventeenth century, the landscape in this area was very different from what it is now. It is estimated that the marshy, boggy, waterlogged land was twenty or thirty feet higher and movement across it was very difficult.

Today as I stand on the flood bank, warily watching a herd of calves that are grazing their way towards me, Ely Cathedral is standing to the north, rising above its collar of green trees. The work on the present cathedral started around 1083. In Hereward's time the buildings on the highest point of the Isle were those of a rich monastery that preceded the cathedral. The course of the river was similar to where it is now but it is likely that the river running through marshland was a different river to the wide Great Ouse which now flows between flood banks. Before the drainage of the Fens this area consisted of marsh and bogs. There were no flood banks to protect this drained and farmed area where now the oil seed rape lies limply behind me waiting to be harvested and in the low lying fertile fields across the river a small army of workers pick and pack celery. It looks like a small village has suddenly appeared. In the corner are caravans and vehicles, progressing slowly along the lines of celery are the tractors and then behind them the pickers passing the vegetables to a mobile packing station.

They work late into the night, floodlights illuminate the workers and I am lulled to sleep by the background drone of farm machinery.

Gnomes

I'm missing my garden. I may have acres of countryside outside my front door and I may be able to set up my chair and table and read or dine by the riverside but it is not the same as having a place to potter and weed and prune. I miss cutting the grass and the evocative smell of a newly mown lawn. I miss watching the new season's shoots and trying to remember what I planted there. I miss growing my own herbs and vegetables. I even miss those nasty, pointy-nosed things that decimated my rocket before I got a chance to eat it.

I may not have a garden but I have a roof. If I eliminate the area needed for the boat hook, the boat pole, a plank, two bikes, a spare bag of coal and the various tools that I have left there when I have been trying to do some running repairs, I have an area of thirty foot by six foot on which to cultivate my pots of plants. I did have a few pots last year but a combination of low bridges and a harsh winter has seen them off.

But this is a new season, a new start. I am going to concentrate on edibles, none of this pretty flower nonsense, if it can't go into my stomach it's not going onto my roof. I am planning on an array of herbs, lettuces, chard, spinach, bush tomatoes, chillies and peppers and who knows if those nasty, pointy-nosed things can't make it to the roof of the boat then I might even be able to grow some rocket. I expect to be able to feed myself and, in a grandiose lady of the manor way, to distribute the surplus to the poor and needy of the boating community.

I needed containers, compost, plants and seeds. The plants and seeds aren't a problem; I can cycle to the garden centre and put them in my bike basket. At a push and at the risk of injuring passers-by I may even be able to manage a few long containers but the transporting of heavy bags of compost is going to be more difficult.

I have a solution. I moored the boat as near to a road as I could and went forth to borrow a car. The Fellow Traveller was moored nearby and I reckoned he owed me a few favours. He didn't think he owed me any favours but he reluctantly agreed to lend me his car for the afternoon. His parting words were, 'This key is the only one I've got, don't lose it.' As if I would.

I went to the Garden Centre in Horningsea to buy the necessary ingredients for the most productive and envied roof garden on the waterways. I selected the herbs and the containers and a 30 litre bag of compost and put them on a trolley and set off to find a till where I could pay for them.

Notcutts Garden Centre has obviously decided that if it takes customers on a long meandering trail through all the departments by the time they get to the tills their trolleys will not only contain the tray of petunias and the plastic window box they came for but will also include the sweaters, books, indoor plants, a wardrobe and two flop-eared rabbits that they couldn't resist on buying.

Give me a wonky trolley laden with a heavy bag of compost and pots of herbs, provide a long trek past the Edinburgh Wool Shop, the book stall, the stand of artfully arranged ceramics, pine furniture and very useful but obscure household items and the only additional things I acquire are a foul temper and a vow never to shop there again. Three quarters of the way through the centre, getting more irritable by the minute I gave up fighting the trolley and let it go its own way. It promptly did a sharp right turn, ploughed into a display of garden gnomes and demolished the lot.

'Don't worry love, I'll deal with this,' said the helpful assistant.

I left him righting the gnomes and I went on my way past the decorative egg cups and the bunches of silk flowers and arrived at the tills two hours after I'd set off. I paid, left, opened the car, unloaded the trolley and there at the bottom of the trolley serenely asleep under a red and white toadstool was a bearded gnome. I checked my receipt and it turned out I'd paid £13.99 for this Notcutts escapee. I picked him up and, because it is the only way in, I went back through the garden centre, past The Edinburgh Wool Shop, the book stall, the display of garden gnomes (once again upright) and all the other paraphernalia to eventually reach the tills. I returned the gnome and got my money back and went back to the car, which I'd left open, and then I couldn't find the keys. I searched the car, emptied the boot, ripped out carpets, felt down backs of seats, crawled on the ground looking underneath the car and still there was no sign of them.

I went back through all the departments selling everything that nobody in their right mind could ever need or want and checked at the tills but I hadn't left them there either.

Notcutts was closing for the night so I had to phone my son to come and collect me and give me a lift back to the boat. I had to leave the car in the car park, locked in behind a high fence. I also had to get into grovel mode and go and tell the Fellow Traveller that I had returned without his car but looking on the bright side although it was inaccessible and immobile it was safe behind locked gates. It turned out that he'd lied to me (no change there then) and he did have another key, a key with a bend in it but there was a chance it would work. Either that or jam in the lock and mess up the car completely.

I told the whole sorry story to Jessica.

'You took the gnome back!'

'Yes.'

'Don't you know gnomes can't face rejection.'

'But he was asleep, how did he know he'd been rejected?'

'Even sleeping gnomes are vindictive, no wonder your car keys went missing.'

The next morning Jessica drove me back to Notcutts Garden Centre. Taking a compass, map and enough food and drink for the journey I set off on the relentless trail through all departments, only stopping at the display of garden gnomes where my erstwhile friend was snoozing peaceably on the bottom shelf.

'Sorry mate,' I said 'but it was for your own good

you wouldn't have liked sleeping on a steel roof in all weathers.'

At the tills I was told that nobody had found my car keys even though the diligent staff had searched thoroughly. I went back to the car, prepared to use the wonky key, opened the boot and there was the original key, in full view, lying on a ledge.

I can only assume that my apology to the sleeping gnome had worked and he'd decided to remove the Gnomic Shield of Invisibility that had been covering the key.

So the moral of the story is, 'Don't Mess With The Gnomes!' Either that or take better care of the car keys.

An Accident

The purchase of the flat is completed, my few remaining bits of tat and boxes of books have been moved into the loft, my daughter is safely installed and a tenant has been found for the spare room. There's no room for me and I'm committed to keeping my equity in the property for at least another four years (or make my daughter homeless) so I better get used to the idea of living on a boat. There is no work on the horizon, my plants are on the roof, the tank is full of diesel. I've run out of excuses for hanging around in East Anglia. Just one more farewell cruise and I will definitely be setting off for the canals.

I ended up going back to St Ives. I didn't intend to return to St Ives. The plan was for friends to come on board for the cruise along the Old West River onto the other bit of the Great Ouse and stop at the Pike and Eel, about five miles upriver in Needingworth, in the evening. They would be picked up from the pub by other friends and the following day my son and his girlfriend would come along and we'd have a farewell Sunday lunch in the pub and then do the return journey to Ely. On the Monday I'd set sail and head down the Great Ouse to Denver across to the Middle Levels up the Nene down the Northampton Arm and then I'd decide whether to turn left or right. St Ives wasn't on the itinerary but plans don't go to plan and stuff happens.

Due to gnome related incidents we set off late and Judith and David went missing and couldn't be contacted to tell them of the re-arranged schedule. Terry and Di turned up and the Fellow Traveller came along as well because he thought the least I owed him after all the trauma with the car was a boat ride, a lunch and a few drinks. Already late we were further delayed when the Fellow Traveller took the tiller and two minutes later grounded us on a mud bank on the Old West River. I went through my routine of deep drawn in breath: long drawn out, 'Tut tut tut': eyebrows raised. I wearily took the tiller to extricate us. At the next bend I managed to ground us even more effectively. So after getting the passengers to jump up and down on the left hand side of the bow and getting the pole out and much pushing and shoving we were freed from the mud and proceeded upriver even more behind schedule.

We did manage to contact Judith and David and we picked them up at Earith. We motored on down the river and all the moorings at the Pike and Eel were occupied which I thought was a pain because by then I was fed-up of driving. My visitors couldn't care less about the lack of moorings because they'd got stuck into the food and wine and were merrily carousing in the bow of the boat. And we motored on further and they were getting merrier and I could hear their laughter drifting back towards me in my lonely position at the helm. I knew I should have bought a boat with a cruiser stern then they would all be back here with me instead of partying sixty feet away at the front of the boat. The merrier they got the grumpier I got.

At Holywell all the moorings were occupied by widely spaced river cruisers and the man on the boat moored at the end of the line shouted, 'I'd moor up if I were you, that lot in the front are finishing all the food and wine,' and I replied in the manner which suited my mood to the effect that I would have liked to moor up but because of the selfish way people in cruisers moored their boats I couldn't fit my long boat in between all their poxy little bits of plastic. For good measure I added a few words which suggested he try sex and travel and cast doubts about his brain capacity and his parentage. My comments were totally unladylike and totally uncalled for and I found them totally satisfying.

Then one of the drunks at the front spotted moorings outside the Ferryboat Inn and we tied up and I found out that they had indeed drunk all the wine and eaten all the food so we went to the pub where their befuddled brains tried to remember where their cars were and then realised they weren't in a fit state to drive them. They wondered, in a haphazard sort of way how were they going to get home because the people picking them up were waiting for us at the Pike and Eel in a SMS black hole. Eventually we co-ordinated cars and pick-ups and I got rid of them and crawled into bed. The next day I wasn't where Alex and Jo had expected me to be so they were a bit late arriving and we spent too long over Sunday lunch which meant the lock at Earith would be closed before we got there. So I decided to go to St Ives, although for the life of me I can't remember why I went to St Ives instead of just staying where I was.

Then the weather was bad, wet and windy and I was offered, unexpectedly, a couple of days work so I decided I'd stay in St Ives a bit longer and set off on the following Sunday. The Queen of Prevarication reigns once more.

On that Saturday morning in early June, in preparation for the big journey, alone, I did what I should have done when I first set off as a single handed sailor; I bought a life-jacket. Two hours later when I fell in the river I wasn't wearing it. It was still in the bag on the kitchen bench.

The general consensus of opinion was that I was an accident waiting to happen. Maybe it was fortunate that I'd managed to avoid the dunking until the weather was warm and the river was tepid.

I was stepping out of the boat, bucket in hand, to water my precious new plants. The last two days of hot dry weather had meant that the river had subsided and left the boat too loosely moored; I'd meant to tighten it up but you know how it is other far more important things had got in the way. I was busy looking at the bottom of my leaky bucket instead of looking where I was going. I strode over the large gap between bank and boat and my foot slipped on the uneven bank. I felt an intense pain in my knee and then the coldness of the water. How I got from the bank into the river is a total blank. Shocked, I surfaced; I was neatly sandwiched between the boat and the bank, chest deep in muddy water, green weed dangling down my forehead, a howling pain in my left leg and the bucket still clasped in my right hand.

183

A couple on the footpath about ten feet from my boat walked past. 'Good Afternoon,' they said cheerily, and marched on their way. It wasn't until later that I wondered about that bright, 'Good Afternoon,' directed at a shocked woman, grimacing in pain, decorated with mud and weed, standing chest deep in muddy water. Was it a regular occurrence to see women in the water? Did they think I'd gone in there deliberately to do some running repairs to the hull? After all they were close enough to see me fall in, and I was still clutching that bucket. Maybe my descent to the depths was a graceful step, turn and slide rather than the inelegant spectacle of flaying arms and legs that I imagined it to be.

Or maybe one muttered to the other, 'Ignore her. We don't want to get involved, we'll only have to help her out and she's wet and dirty. You've got your new trainers and jeans on, if you get grass stains on them they'll never come out. We'll pretend nothing's wrong, we'll just say, 'Good Afternoon' and walk passed.' And so they said, 'Good Afternoon' and walked on their way and I just stood there in a soggy painful silence, watching their retreating backs.

As the pain subsided slightly, soothed by the coolness of the water, and the dizziness faded I thought I had better find a way out of the river. The bank was sticky mud interspersed with a few nettles; one of my legs was useless and I was feeling queasy and woozy. I tried pulling myself out but it was hopeless; the bank was too high and I couldn't get a purchase on the slimy surface.

There was a cruiser moored in front of my boat.

Three people were on board, drinking wine, chatting and laughing having a pleasant Saturday afternoon; a bit of a contrast to the way my own Saturday afternoon was panning out. I tried to attract their attention with a few feeble, 'Hellos,' and polite, 'Excuse mes'. That didn't work. Then I did a full throttle 'HELP!' That brought them running. One assessed the situation, the depth of the water and the weight of the stranded object and decided that two men would be needed to haul me out. He called for his son to come and help, the lad lumbered over, a strapping teenager with a, 'do I have to,' expression on his face. The father decided that they would each grab hold of an arm each and yank me out. I was already feeling pretty stupid at having fallen in the water in the first place and the prospect of the added ignominy of being hauled out of the river by a bald headed man and a stroppy, spotty teenager galvanised me into action. I grabbed a chunk of grass and levered myself out. I sprawled across the bank, lay there breathing heavily and dripping and then managed to shuffle onto my boat.

So now I knew the answer to that frequently asked question, 'What do you do if you have an accident?' Well, when you have crawled back on the boat first of all you throw up, then remove wet and muddy clothes, step into a hot shower (and No Martin I didn't have a heart attack) then wrap up in a duvet and go to bed feeling exceedingly sorry for yourself. Then you have a good cry. When the shaking and tears stop you ring everybody within a fifty mile radius (starting with nearest and dearest), only to find they have gone out for the day and left their mobile phones behind on the kitchen table. Then you thank God for the lovely people on the boat moored behind that come along bearing cups of tea, sympathy and paracetamol. Later in the evening when the pain in the knee is becoming unbearable you ring NHS Direct who tell you to ring the ambulance service which you duly do. The ambulance co-ordinator then decides your injuries are not life-threatening (what does she know about it anyway) and therefore the ambulance will pick you up when they can, which could be in about four hours' time, and when you have been treated you will have to find your own way home. At that point the realisation that you could be in A & E at midnight on a Saturday night when the England team is playing their first World Cup match makes the pain suddenly seem bearable and you decide to swallow the last of the paracetamol and wait until morning.

I had to rely on the ambulance the following day because I couldn't think how, even if I summoned help, I could get off the boat with only one working leg and the other one shooting with pain if I tried even the smallest of movements. I was moored alongside a grassy bank and the nearest place to park a rescue vehicle was about five hundred yards away. The ambulance service required a post code to come and find me. I didn't know the post code of the bit of bank I was moored against but I knew where I was, I was next to the Dolphin Hotel. Didn't they know where that was? But they needed a post code so they could set their sat navs. 'Don't they have maps as well?' I asked but it appeared that they had gone high tech and had problems dealing with low tech patients.

The ambulance crew did arrive even without the help of a post code and they couldn't think how I would get off the boat with one working leg and one shooting with pain if I tried even the smallest of movements. The door to the boat is very narrow so they wouldn't have been able to get me and the stretcher off the boat without tipping it sideways, and therefore tipping me back into the river. If one of them propped me up it would have been difficult for two of us to squeeze through that door. In addition there are three steep steps to get out and a big gap between bank and boat. They were thinking of ringing for an extra ambulance crew to come along and help but they still couldn't think how four people would manage it.

In the end I shuffled on my bum up the steps, the ambulance crew helped me onto the gunwales of the boat, then pulled the boat as near to the bank as possible and I did a Fosbury flop from the boat to the bank. After that it was easy, they loaded me onto a stretcher and wheeled me across the bumpy grass, down the steps and across the cobbled pavement to where the ambulance waited. By this time quite a few spectators had gathered but I didn't get much sympathy, because of living the open air life I looked disgustingly healthy. I did try to point out that every jolt of the stretcher was jarring my injured knee but it seemed that nobody felt my pain.

I may have got the following facts wrong, I wasn't in the right frame of mind to absorb complex information but as I understood it the ambulance had come from Peterborough (about twenty miles away), because the local stations weren't manned until after 10am on a Sunday morning. So please note citizens of Cambridgeshire don't have heart attacks or serious car accidents on a Sunday morning because the ambulance may be a long time arriving. Then after being loaded into the ambulance I was asked where I wanted to go. Momentarily I wondered if I'd rung the wrong number and called for a taxi instead of ambulance. I looked around and the interior of the vehicle had all the paraphernalia associated with an ambulance and the two crew members were wearing neat navy blue uniforms and were running through routine blood pressure tests. It transpired that under new NHS directives I could choose which hospital I wanted to be delivered to. I assume the choice was restricted to local hospitals and that I couldn't choose to be taken to A & E in Kendal because I fancied a scenic view from the window.

As I didn't have my Good Hospitals Guide with me to check which one was best for dealing with buggered up knees I asked to be delivered to the nearest one. I put it down to the stress of the situation that I didn't do the sensible thing and ask to be taken to Addenbrooke's hospital in Cambridge.

I was taken to Hinchingbrooke Hospital in Huntingdon, wheeled into a sparkling clean room and transferred to a trolley. The nurse propped my leg up with rolled blankets and for the first time since I had had the accident it felt reasonably comfortable. The nurse left and I caught up with some sleep. Two hours later I was woken up by another nurse who asked me what the doctor had said. I told him I hadn't seen a doctor, so he went off to find one and I went back to sleep. Eventually I was examined, dispatched for an X-ray and it was decided I had not broken any bones, I'd probably ruptured the cruciate ligament but it was difficult to say because the knee was so swollen. I was bandaged up, given crutches and sent home. I knew my son was away for the day so I rang the Fellow Traveller and he willingly came over to collect me.

I was told to come back in a week's time, and in the meantime to put as little weight as possible on the damaged leg. If you only have one good leg a boat isn't a bad place to be, four hops to the loo, ten hops to the kettle and narrow corridors mean there is always something to hold onto. It was impossible to get off the boat but I could sit on the seat in the bow and talk to people passing by, read my books, listen to the radio and chat to the ducks.

I listened to an article on Woman's Hour that said we have all become, 'less neighbourly'. The friendliness, the popping in for cups of tea, the mutual support in times of hardship or sadness had all become things of the past. The interviewee puts this down to the transient nature of our modern society. People who move away from their communities don't put down roots and don't get a chance to know their neighbours and don't have a sense of responsibility towards them.

I have to report that here on the river, in this most transient of communities, neighbourliness is alive and well. I am overwhelmed by the kindness and concern of people mooring up for short periods who offer sympathy and help. I have talked to more people in my short sojourn here than in my years of living in a village outside of Cambridge. I have exchanged mobile phone numbers with strangers who insist I call them if I need shopping or help moving the boat.

A man on his way to Bedford brought a bottle of wine to share.

I have had regular, 'poppers in' making sure I am coping with immobility and a man with a dog comes by every day to check if I need anything and to try to sell me an annual subscription to Canal Boat Rescue. He may be working on the principle that an injured woman is going to be vulnerable to his sales spiel. His main selling point seems to be that if I'd been a member of Canal Boat Rescue when I had had this accident I could have got discounted car hire. He's ignoring the fact that I can't even walk to a car let alone drive it. But not to worry he's a nice man and his dog is friendly.

I have another regular visitor, a little white duck with a black stripe on her nose and her nine ducklings, four brown ducklings and five yellow ducklings, little scraps of fluff with pinprick black eyes, scooting around their mother, fighting for the scraps of bread, piping shrilly when they are separated from her. They rest on the bank opposite clustered around her while she tries ineffectually to fit them all under her wings. They are endlessly entertaining.

But best of all are my next door neighbours, Maureen and Eric, stranded on this riverbank with a broken engine. They make me cups of tea, shop, bring me strawberries and cream and most importantly they make me laugh.

News of my predicament has flowed up and down river, when boaters chat on the riverbank they have to have something to chat about and some lone, elderly woman boater who has fallen in the river and damaged her leg is as good a topic of conversation as any.

One calm evening when sounds drift clearly across the water I hear two couples moored on the opposite bank discussing me. It appears that instead of a brief dunk in water shallow enough to stand up in, an undignified scrabble up the bank and a torn ligament I fell into deep water had to be retrieved by boat and I have a fractured leg. No doubt by the time each couple go their opposite ways along the river the story will be further embellished. In St Neots the talk will be of helicopters scrambled in a life and death rescue attempt and at the lock at Earith the tale will be of an unfortunate woman who has had to have both legs amputated after being trapped between boats.

I lie here doing nothing much because I can't do anything much. I am enjoying indolence. And the weather is good. And the view is pleasant. From my vantage point in the bow where I sit with my leg propped up I look across the large water meadow to the village of Hemingford Grey, where the spire of the church pokes up behind the dark green swathe of trees, I watch dog walkers and the ramblers and the changing light and the setting sun. My visitor the little white duck now only has five ducklings; three brown and two yellow. What has happened to the others?

'Pike,' says Eric.

'Rats,' says the Canal Boat Rescue man.

'Sparrow hawks,' says a dog walker.

'Swans will kill anything,' says a man fishing.

'Herons,' say the two women in a river cruiser. Herons? Surely not. Herons have long thin necks specifically designed to swallow fish surely ducklings, all feet feathers and bills would get stuck, after all they can't chew their prey first. It's catch a fish and swallow. I can't believe the beautiful, stately herons would stoop to taking pretty little ducklings for their lunch.

On the left of the boat are the banqueting rooms of the hotel and it is the wedding season. I have become an expert on wedding garb. For the benefit of prospective wedding guests, high heels are only attractive if you know how to walk in them and even if you can walk elegantly in them don't attempt to walk across a lawn. Gladiator sandals are never attractive however well you walk. Tight skirts only work on the very slim and frills should only be worn by bridesmaids. Fascinators only fascinate because of their awfulness. Most fascinators look as if a dead bird has suddenly fallen from the skies and landed on the unsuspecting head of the wedding guest. Stick to big hats ladies, they're more flattering.

My favourite wedding was the one at which groom and best man wore kilts and the bride was piped in. Later in the afternoon when the bride and groom had retired to their room for a break before the evening festivities, the bride was leaning out of the window waving her wedding ring at passing walkers shouting, 'Look I'm married, I'm married.'

I lie in the bow, head and knee propped on cushions, and watch the world of St Ives pass by. Somewhere within me is a residue of a northern working ethic. The residue has never been large enough to make me put down the book, get off the sofa and do the house-work but it is just the right size to cause a slight guilt when I am laying on the sofa with a book when there is work to be done. With a leg that needs to be rested I can laze in the sun without the company of my little nugget of guilt niggling away.

Enforced leisure really is rather pleasant.

St Ives

'They're blowing up the bridge today,' said Maureen.

That's not very nice of them I think. The 15th century bridge in St Ives is very attractive, it's made of stone and has an exceptionally charming and decorative little chapel built onto one side of it. Evidently it is one of only four bridges in the country that have buildings on them. It would be a shame to blow it up.

Then I remember that it is the 900th anniversary of the founding of St Ives and so the blowing up of the bridge must be something to do with the birthday celebrations. I've seen the signs for a re-enactment of a Civil War battle. It is a re-enactment of a battle that never took place. Oliver Cromwell, the local lad made good, or made bad depending which side you're on, did indeed blow up two of the arches of the bridge and replace them with a wooden drawbridge in an attempt to stop the royalist troops. The royalist troops never invaded. They contented themselves with doing some rape and pillage ten miles away in Huntingdon and didn't bother with St Ives. Blowing a hole in the bridge ruined its symmetry, the replacement arches don't quite match, but it probably kept the citizens of St Ives safe from Royalist armies and stopped battalions of Royalists rampaging through their town. Today the citizens of St Ives won't be able to rest as peaceably for at 11am the bridge will be blown up and the battle will commence. The Royalist hoards will march into the town and the skirmishes will spill into the streets and deadly hand to hand fighting will take place in the doorways of Boots and W H Smith and in the afternoon the armies and their followers will decamp to the golf course and fire off cannon and shout a lot and charge at each other. A bit of historical accuracy about sites of battles is not going to get in the way of the hordes of the Sealed Knot disrupting the Saturday shoppers of St Ives and having fun.

At 10am a river cruiser ties up on the opposite bank and four roundheads and a cavalier get off. They didn't have the appearance of well-honed fighting men, they are more round bellied than round headed. If they'd come on a route march from Naseby they must have stopped at a few Little Chefs on the way.

At 11am prompt there was a loud bang and a flash; smoke billowed; the smell of cordite filled the air. The pigeons rose in a panic stricken flurry above the town. The little white duck and her ducklings, which I now noted numbered only four, zoomed around the corner into the calm and safety of our cut. Only the platoon of swans remained serene and unperturbed and floated through the clouds of smoke towards the crowds gathering on the quayside hoping for rich food pickings. Still unable to walk or leave the boat I hopped to the back deck to try and see what was happening. I could only catch glimpses of the events on the bridge. Visible over the parapets were a row of staffs and the tips of muskets and the glint of sunlight on metal. There was a lot of indistinct shouting. Then there was a shout of, 'In the name of the King' which didn't go down very well with the carriers of the staffs and muskets and the wearers of the round glinting helmets so they shouted a lot more and there were more bangs and the smell of cordite drifted across and the pigeons once more rose in terror.

Then on the bridge appeared a row of mounted cavaliers with floppy feathered hats and swords and muskets, amidst more shouting and bangs they progressed across the bridge followed by foot soldiers. From my vantage point I could only see the hats of the foot soldiers moving across the bridge. And nice hats they were too; all velvet and feathers. The sound of fighting moved away and then came in sporadic bursts from the centre of town. In a gap between buildings across the river I could see and hear a pipe and fife band marching along The Waits and heading out of town. The Roundheads were in retreat, the Royalists had captured St Ives. I wondered if the Roundheads would get their chance to win when the afternoon battle took place at the Golf Club, although if they started churning up the greens and leaving musket balls on the fairway I wouldn't fancy the chance of either army against a battalion of angry golfers armed with Number 4 irons.

At 1pm the four roundheads and one cavalier reappeared and sat by their boat drinking beer and eating sandwiches and they were joined by a seventeenth century serving wench smoking a cigarette and drinking a glass of wine.

I have always been rather derogatory about Civil

War enactment groups. I've put them in the same category as train spotters and twitchers and people who sit on canal banks all day catching small fish and then throwing them back in. But I was impressed by this battle in St Ives. The organisation needed to get hundreds of foot soldiers, marching bands and mounted cavaliers stomping around a small market town without causing harm to the locals was impressive. Who planned it? Some general I suppose. Who choreographed the hand-to-hand fighting in the doorways of Boots? Was it just a free-form scrap or did the combatants have to work to a set routine? Who decided who won the imaginary battles? Did they sometimes decide that it was the turn of the Royalist army to win at Naseby? Did the participants sustain injuries? Was there lots of blood?

I thought I'd rather like to join one of the Civil War re-enactment societies. As long as I'm allowed to go into battle, I don't want to be a serving wench left behind in the tents making the sandwiches. I want to brandish a sword and fire a musket and if somebody could lend me a horse I'd like to be mounted. Of course I'd want to be a Royalist, my sympathies and political views are definitely on the side of the Parliamentarians but the Royalists have the best hats.

Given the choice between an unflattering inverted chamber pot and a flowing concoction of velvet and feathers and ribbons there is no contest. Never mind the political affiliations, just give me the best headgear.

Hobbling

Ten days after the accident I returned to the hospital and had the bandage removed and my leg didn't drop off. The doctor tutted a lot about the person who had put the bandage on too tight and thereby caused me extra swelling and discomfort. I just admired the multi-coloured hues of my leg. I was told to rest the leg and come back in six weeks' time when the swelling would have gone down and I can have scans to decide what damage had been done. I was given a very impressive blue leg brace. I notice that Rio Ferdinand is featured on the front pages of the newspapers wearing a similar one. So now I have something in common with a famous footballer, both of us have injuries to our ligaments and neither of us is going to captain England for their World Cup matches.

The leg brace makes my leg feel more secure and I am now able to hobble around and given a few hours of slow movement accompanied by a lot of groans I can get off the boat.

Apart from the need for protection I have occasionally thought of getting a dog for the social aspect. I notice that people with dogs talk to each other and I thought it would be a way of making new acquaintances. For the last ten days I have sat here in the bow of my boat and observed the stream of dog walkers that come through the squeaky gate onto the meadows and my theory that dog walkers talk to each other has been confirmed. I've also noticed that once the mandatory comment about the weather has been dispensed with the only topic of conversation between dog walkers is dogs. I don't want to spend the rest of my life talking about dogs so that is another good reason not to get one.

Having a large blue brace strapping that stretches from hip to ankle, and hobbling along with the aid of crutches has a similar effect to walking a dog in that people who feel an affinity with women with a bad leg do stop and talk. Except that the conversation isn't about dogs it's about knees. Before I have reached the bridge I have had a dozen accounts of knee injuries and knee operations and the tales of how long it took to get over that operation and what a difference it made to their lives and the pain. Oh we can't forget the pain. Are you in pain? Yes I'm in pain but I'm beginning to believe that the most painful part is listening to the details of all those operations. I was stopped (actually I was moving so slowly it was difficult to discern if I was stopped or still in motion) by an Italian man who told me that in Italy the physiotherapy starts before the operation so that the muscles are built up in readiness to support the weakness caused by surgery. He asked me if I'd had physiotherapy first. I did think it was a good idea but told him that in the few seconds between leaving the bank and hitting the water I didn't have the time to do twenty leg lifts and twelve knee stretches. He nodded in agreement. I think my sarcasm failed to pass the language barrier.

Despite having to listen to endless gory details about

accidents and operations it is good to be almost mobile again. I'd never thought of St Ives as an exciting place, as a centre of hedonist pleasure but compared to the bow of a boat overlooking a large meadow it holds endless delights. There's a market and a library and a Waitrose and a museum and a nature reserve on Holts Island which I never get to visit because it's always closed when I hobble over there. There's the hotel with the wide-screen television which shows World Cup football matches every evening except when the local Women's Institute hold a quiz. There are good pubs and a couple of excellent Indian restaurants. It even has an off-licence that sells hundreds of types of whisky. I don't like whisky but I limp in regularly to look at bottles of whisky with names that evoke memories of remote Scottish islands and highlands and heather and mists.

I find a bit of medieval wall that was part of a priory where a stone coffin was discovered in the 11th century. The Abbot of Ramsey decided, with little real evidence, that this coffin contained the remains of a Persian Bishop. This find precipitated the renaming of the village of Slepe to St Ives. I have plenty of time to stand in front of this bit of wall in a scruffy back street and ponder on the relative merits of the name St Ives and Slepe. As a name St Ives has more gravitas but it's always getting confused with that other one in Cornwall that has all the wives and cats and kittens. I remember a phone call to my elderly cantankerous Aunt from a building society in St Ives when I was trying to manage her financial affairs.

200

'Miss Wilson it's the Halifax in St Ives we have your niece here…'

'What's she doing in St Ives she hasn't told me she was going to Cornwall. Tell her if she goes away on holiday the least I expect is a postcard, tell her when she gets back to come and see me immediately …'

Due to my aunt's deafness the conversation went on for a long time and her booming voice could be heard all over the branch much to the amusement of the other customers. Would it have been any easier if St Ives was still called Slepe?

'Miss Wilson it's the Halifax here, your niece is in Slepe.'

'What's she doing asleep at this time of the day she should be looking after those two children of hers not sleeping ….'

As soon as you open the door of the Norris Museum in St Ives your nostrils are assailed by the smell of fust. The fusty smell that permeates churches and ancient stately homes, the fusty smell that speaks of old material and documents and things. And the Norris Museum has lots of things. A plastic Ichthyosaur dangles from the ceiling and there are rows of old fashioned glass cases containing stones and bones, pipes and bottles and the work of prisoners captured during the Napoleonic War. I thought how boring and limped around the glass cases looking at the bits of bone and details of lace-making, old bottles, Roman jugs, and read the labels and then gradually became absorbed in this odd collection of memorabilia, ancient items and fossilised cats found in walls.

There is a large display of photographs, ancient skates and information about the ice-skating that has taken place for hundreds of years at nearby Bury Fen and the families, both local men and men from Holland, who dominated the sport.

There's a smaller display case about the Civil War. I think the collector of the artefacts must have been a Royalist. The information panels tell of the Royalist victory and ransacking of Huntingdon and that King Charles may have passed north of St Ives when he was fleeing. Of Oliver Cromwell, the local landowner and MP there is only a small mention.

The opinions about Oliver Cromwell vary wildly and have fluctuated over the years since his death. On his death he was given a state funeral. Two years later the body was dug up and was taken to Tyburn where the corpse was hung drawn and quartered and then decapitated. His head was on display for many years on a spike outside Westminster Hall and is now thought to be buried in his old college, Sydney Sussex, in Cambridge.

The statue of Oliver Cromwell in St Ives wasn't erected until 1901 although the rather fetching orange and white traffic cone that now sits on his head is most likely a recent addition. The statue of Oliver Cromwell in Parliament Square was erected at a similar time. It was erected in St Ives because the more royalist town of Huntingdon, Cromwell's birthplace, refused to commemorate him. At the end of Victoria's reign perhaps the public were getting rather bored with the monarchy and this was assumed to be the trigger to reassess the heritage left by Oliver Cromwell.

I went to the Oliver Cromwell museum in Huntingdon. It is in a small sixteenth century building that used to be the grammar school. It was the school that Oliver Cromwell attended, as did Samuel Pepys. On the wall is a painting by Sir Peter Lely which purports to be the painting which caused Cromwell to make the famous statement, 'Paint me warts and all'. At Compton Verney there is a miniature of Oliver Cromwell exquisitely painted by Samuel Cooper that also professes to be the origin of that saying. Maybe Cromwell said, 'Paint me warts and all,' to everybody who painted him or maybe he never said it at all.

Cromwell is famous for his puritan way of life and for his plain dress. In the centre of the room in Huntingdon is the hat that he wore to the dissolution of Parliament in 1653. It is a felt hat once black now faded to a rusty brown. It's a plain hat, it doesn't have any feathers, it hasn't got turned brims or flamboyant decorations. It is also an extremely large hat. It must be one of the largest hats I've seen. I think the wearer of the hat was very aware of the impression he was making and probably had an ego as big as the brim.

Leaving St Ives

I peer out of my window and eyeball a middle-aged couple peering in. They smile sheepishly and mouth through the window, 'We were just admiring your boat.' Where Rea is concerned I'm a sucker for admiration so I invite them in to have a look around. A conducted tour of a narrow boat doesn't take long, 'Here's the sitting room and this is the dining table which converts into a double bed. Here's the bathroom and it even has a small bath which I've never had the courage to lower my big bottom into in case I get stuck. Here's the bedroom and through this door is the engine bit which has a washing machine which never works because the batteries aren't strong enough to power it.' That's it. Tour over. Then we stand and look at each other and the visitors make clucking noises about how nice it all is and how compact and then rack their brains for salient questions to ask. If I am showing people around who are thinking of living aboard I show them all the nooks and crannies which have been designed for storage. I am quite ashamed of this because I have never accumulated enough stuff to fill them all. I feel I should be saying, '.. and this is where I store my tools and I keep my bee-keeping equipment under the bow and under the bed I have all my linen and …' but on Rea most of these cleverly designed storage spaces are empty. It is the complaint of live-aboards that they never have enough storage space for belongings, I feel I have let the side down by not having enough belongings for the storage spaces.

This couple are impressed with Rea, they enthuse, they love her. I warm to them. They admire the teak panelling and the way the light dances across it and enhances the grain of the wood. I put the kettle on and check that the biscuits haven't grown a layer of mould.

'It's just like that caravan we used to have in Skegness isn't it?' the woman says.

'Yes,' he agrees 'I was thinking that. The way the table collapses into a bed and all this Formica on the walls reminds me of Skeggie.'

Whaaat!! Formica!! They're comparing my finely crafted, wood panelled beautiful boat to a plastic caravan in Skegness. I take the kettle off the hob and shepherd them hurriedly towards the door.

As they leave I look across the cut, the little white duck is on the bank opposite and there is no sign of her last duckling. She is snuggled up against a multi-coloured drake. The tart. If she is planning on starting a second brood I hope she looks after them better than the first.

I'm fed-up of being stranded in St Ives and I want to get moving again. The leg is still painful and encased in the blue brace so I won't be able to manage the locks by myself and if I fall in the brace will probably counter-act the effect of my new, unused life-jacket, weigh me down and I will sink without trace. I will need help. I know a man who still owes me a few favours (although the balance of favours is rapidly starting to tilt in the opposite direction). I phone the Fellow Traveller and he is happy to come and help me move off.

Half a mile downriver we get to St Ives lock. He gets off. I expect him to take the bow rope and tie up the boat but he doesn't take the rope so I drift away from the pontoon. I shout at him for not stepping off with the rope, he shouts at me for not throwing him the centre rope. He goes to open the lock gates but they appear to open by themselves; struggling to hold the boat against the force of the weir and the wind I wait for the occupants to come out; nobody appears and the lock seems empty; I head into the lock and a narrow boat materialises from nowhere and we are on collision course. I put my boat into hard reverse and shoot out backwards, they squeeze past with much head shaking and eyebrow raising. I'd forgotten that the lock at St Ives has a sort of alcove in which boats can lurk unseen. The Fellow Traveller is leaning on the lock gate watching all this happen without attempting to indicate to me that it's not safe to enter the lock. I glower and make a few salient remarks. He ignores me, closes the downriver gates and goes to open the upriver gates then remembers that he hasn't got the windlass with him. I throw one up to him it bounces against the wall and falls into the lock. He makes a few comments about women's inability to throw. I make a few remarks about men's inability to take essential tools with them. I hand him the spare windlass with a sour smile. Half an hour of travelling together and already we're not speaking. It's just like the old times.

My leg aches so I reluctantly allow the Fellow Traveller to take the tiller and I go and sit in the front of the boat. I rarely get the chance to sit at the front and it

206

is surprising how quiet it all seems and how smoothly we move along. No noisy engines, no smell of diesel, no wrestling with heavy tillers. It is a beautiful day, warm, and the tree-lined banks shelter the boat from the wind. The river flows beyond the open fields into wooded areas that are interspersed with in-filled gravel pits that are now nature reserves. The gravel bed of the river combined with the recent lack of rainfall means the water runs crystal clear and I can look down at layers of fish. Damsel flies, brilliant turquoise needles, dart over the water. A kingfisher sits on a branch of a tree his attention so fixed on the movement of fish in the river that he appears oblivious to a large boat passing by. A dark furry animal scuttles into a hole on the riverbank. I'd like to think it was an otter. Otters are re-establishing themselves and being reintroduced along this stretch of the river but it is more likely that I have seen a mink, beautiful but vicious and fearless little creatures that are destroying the natural wildlife along these banks.

There are three cormorants on the telegraph wires that cross the river. They are stretching their wings out to dry in the morning sun, or are they sunbathing? Whatever they are doing I find this wing stretching a rather endearing habit of cormorants. I always think of cormorants as the ugly cousins of the elegant herons (although technically they are not related). Their necks stick out, their faces are plain and their flight looks flappy and uncoordinated. In addition they are a plain and boring black. On this bright sunlit day, though, when the river is clear and a fourth cormorant dives into the river next to the boat it is to watch a streamlined killing machine streak deeply under the water to catch its prey. Their short wings, which make their flight look clunky, and hook at the end of their bill aid their diving and fish catching abilities. Their ratio of dive to catch is high, I have always noticed that the cormorant is more likely to surface (often a long way from where it dived in) with a fish in its beak rather than without one. The terns which are circling overhead are even more efficient catchers of fish. The herons, on the other hand, seem to stand motionless on the bank for hours with occasional stabs into the water that fail to come up with any fish.

Cormorants became a protected species under the Wildlife and Countryside Act of 1981 and since then their numbers have increased substantially. anglers hate cormorants. They refer to them as the Black Killers. There has been a campaign in the Angling Trust for a dramatic culling of cormorants, especially on the Lea River in Hertfordshire where they have decimated the fish stocks. Personally I think these efficient and fascinating birds should be left alone and I would go as far as to say if the Cormorant and Tern Trust wants to start a campaign to cull canal side anglers then I'm with them all the way.

Four months ago when I came downriver after my winter sojourn at Buckden it was in flood and the fields were still under water and I was concerned that I might miss the course of the river. Now the water levels are low and the sandy banks at the river's edge are exposed. The fields at Bury Fen, between Bottisham and Earith which are flooded every winter are now once more drained and cows graze in the lush water meadows. In cold years when there are several days of sub-zero temperatures these flooded fields turned to sheets of ice. When we lived a couple of miles from here we ventured out of the warm house and watched the local people don the curved bladed outdoor ice-skates to spend hours skating across these flooded, frozen fields. Old men bundled up against the cold, one arm behind the back the other swinging low, were skating as they have done at every opportunity since childhood, children falling over and teenagers were being noisy. Sleds and sleighs and a motley collection of home-made skates and devices for passage across the ice all cluttered Bury Fen. On a winter's day when the afternoon sun was setting casting its orange light over the sheet of ice it looked like a scene from a Breughel painting. I'd brought my children here for many years when the ice was thick enough to walk on. We slid and spectated but we never skated because we didn't have skates. Then I bought a job lot at auction which included three pairs of outdoor skates and looked forward to trying them out. I never got the chance to test my skills as a speed skater because for the next fifteen years the winter temperatures were never low enough for long enough to freeze the flooded fields. Last year when I cleared the house prior to selling it I sent the skates to an Oxfam shop. This winter the fields had been frozen for weeks and the skating conditions were brilliant.

Local people have been skating here for centuries

and for over a hundred years, as the display at the Norris Museum in St Ives had verified. When the weather is below freezing for a number of days and the ice becomes thick enough to hold the skaters the British Speed Skating Championships are held here.

The bank opposite Bury Fen is exposed and forty miles inland a seal and her pup bask on the mud flats. The short stretch of river between Earith Lock and Brownshill Lock is tidal, although here the rise and fall of the tides is minimal. At Earith there are sluice gates which open out onto the Old Bedford River. It stretches from Earith to Denver and it is possible for boats to travel this stretch of water when the tide is falling. The seals must have come down this tidal waterway. The seals are a fixture along this stretch, one of the pubs on the riverbank advertises a seal spotting area. I am told that there are currently five seals on this stretch of the river. I bet the anglers hate them.

As we go into Earith Lock the Fellow Traveller shouts, 'There's a picture of you in this lock.' What fame at last, have I become the pin-up of the waterways system? When I bring the boat in I see the diagram of a woman pushing a boat away from the wall by holding onto the chains at the lock side, of the boat moving away, of the woman arms and legs outstretched falling into the water. So he thinks I look like the example of how to do stupid things on a boat. Huhh.

At Earith the wide Great Ouse stops abruptly. To the west runs the Old West River, to the north run the Old and the New Bedford Rivers which were the original dykes constructed when the drainage of the Fens began.

The Old Bedford was started in 1630 by the Duke of Bedford. He brought in the Dutch engineer Vermuyden and his team to work on the huge project, on the assumption that the Dutch knew a bit about land drainage. All these miles of wide ditches were dug by hand by the Dutch workers, it was a mammoth task and took years. Their influence remains not just in these wide drainage ditches but if you look in the graveyards around these parts you can see gravestones bearing names of Dutch origin and at the nearby village of Over many of the old houses with gable roofs have a Dutch feel to them. The local people violently opposed the drainage of the Fens and Oliver Cromwell, a local Member of Parliament, was popular because he supported them. His support may have had something to do with the fact that the money generated from the reclaimed land was going into the King's coffers. Later, when the money was going into the Parliamentary coffers he changed his mind and supported the land reclamation.

Once through Earith Lock we are on the narrow and winding Old West River which meanders for twenty miles before it re-joins the wide Great Ouse. I'm not sure why it isn't still called the Great Ouse but man has been messing around with the course of these rivers since pre-Roman times so some illogical names and inexplicable watercourses are inevitable.

We both stand at the back of the boat and watch the countryside crawl past. We know this stretch of the river well. We lived in wedded bliss a few miles away from here. I often picked the children up after school to cycle down and picnic on the riverbank, pick blackberries and wave at passing boats. At least I picked blackberries and waved at passing boats the children just whinged because they'd rather have been at home watching the television. From the water it all looks different. We have difficulty recognising landmarks we thought we knew so well. Doesn't Earith Road look different when you're below it rather than on it? Oh here's Flat Bridge, it's almost falling down, there used to be a farm here with dogs that barked at the children. That's the high bank I used to ride the horse along. Is that Queenholme Farm? Look how high those Leylandii have grown. This must be Aldreth High Bridge.

Aldreth High Bridge is the point where Aldreth Causeway crosses the river. In ancient times it was one of only three crossing points, the other two being Earith and Stuntney, onto the Isle of Ely when the Isle of Ely was literally an island surrounded by marshland. William the Conqueror used this route in his pursuit of Hereward the Wake. One story is that he built a causeway across the marshy ground but when his armoured men and horses started to cross their weight caused the causeway to collapse. William built another causeway made of reeds and for good measure employed a witch to rain curses upon the head of Hereward. Hereward retaliated by setting fire to the reeds and in the process burnt the witch to death. He then retreated to the monastery at Ely. In the middle ages the Aldreth Causeway was the main route from Ely to Cambridge and had a toll booth at either end. It has also always been the route taken by Travellers as they progressed from farm to farm as itinerant workers. The seasonal farm labouring and picking is now mainly carried out by Eastern European students. Nowadays the Travelling community is more involved with used car and scrap metal dealing than fruit picking. They still have a large presence here much to the chagrin of local home-owners. At the Willingham end of the causeway it is usual to see three or four caravans camped and there is a large site at Smithy Fen to the east of the causeway which, it is estimated, houses over five hundred people.

I have read blogs written by boaters travelling along the Old West River and they enthuse about the charm, the peace and seclusion of this part of the river and how tranquil the moorings at Aldreth are. I'm not sure I would feel comfortable moored here, not because I'm concerned about the ghosts of long dead Norman legions or burnt out witches but more because I know the causeway as a back route taken by car thieves and joy riders and a regular repository for burnt out vehicles.

After a few more bends we can see Twentypence Bridge ahead of us, after another few bends we can see Twentypence Bridge to our right, then it's on the left but it never gets any nearer. A pair of swans, with four fluffy grey cygnets in tow, glower at us as we pass. We run aground on a sandbank and have to reverse off. It's the same sandbank we hit on our way upriver over six weeks ago, you'd think we would have learned to avoid it. A heron flaps low above our heads. Still

Twentypence Bridge remains in the distance.

Eventually we pass under it. Twentypence Bridge crosses Twentypence Road. There used to be a Twentypence Inn but that has been demolished to make way for housing. The bridge wasn't built until 1910 before that a ferry took people across the river, presumably the fare was twenty pence.

We plod along the twisting Old West River, progress is slow because water levels are low and weed levels are high. The prop is frequently entangled in weed and we have to keep stopping to free it. It's a nasty job lifting the heavy cover to the weed hatch lying down and groping below the water level to free the weed from the propeller. Sadly because of being encased in my leg brace I can't get down into the weed hatch so the Fellow Traveller has to lift the cover and lie on his stomach and put his arm to shoulder level in cold water and grasp the slimy weed and pull it free. Oh dear, what a shame, poor thing I do feel guilty making him do this. Also if he has any open cuts he may get river borne infections or even Weil's disease and that is nasty. Oh dear.

At Stretham an early Victorian pumping station looms in the distance. It is an imposing brick built structure on the south bank of the river. There are many of these old brick built pumping stations scattered across the Fens. They originally housed steam engines and were built to supersede the battalion of windmills that were originally responsible for pumping the water from the land. Due to the drainage the ground level has lowered and the rivers and dykes are now higher than the surrounding fields. To prevent the Fens reverting to their soggy origins water is pumped upwards to the rivers and drainage dykes. Walking by a riverside or on raised banks of the Old Bedford or the Hundred Foot Bank the walker is often twenty feet or more above the fields and has a panoramic view across the countryside. Alternatively it is possible to travel along a sunken, drunken, exhaust shattering Fen road and see in the distance, like a mirage, a boat sailing above the level of the fields.

Much Victorian industrial architecture, like this pumping station, enhances the landscape whilst most modern buildings detract from it. Although in this unbeautiful area of endless fields and ditches I have a theory that any structure, however bland or ugly, provides a focal point and improves the landscape. A march of electricity pylons gives height and scale to the flatness and a cluster of white wind turbines emerging from the mist are a pleasing alternative to the tedium of endless fields of cabbages. When I espouse my views about pylons being a visual plus I don't gain friends amongst the lovers of the Fen landscape. And yes there are lovers of the Fen landscape who enthuse about the wide skies and err.... the wide skies.

Shortly after passing the Stretham Pumping Station we pass a line of moored boats and then the corner where the Fish and Duck pub used to sit and we're back onto the wide waters of the Great Ouse. Ahead of us the wide skies are tinged with pink, illuminating Ely Cathedral where it sits atop the Isle.

It's late when we arrive at Ely, dusk is falling and as I moor up I notice that a few boats along is Eric and Maureen's boat. That makes me happy. It's good to see familiar and friendly faces.

Leaving Ely

Single handed sailing requires a degree of agility for the clambering onto roofs and the climbing of ladders to get onto the side of locks. At the best of times I am not the most agile of people. This is not the best of times. I have a bad leg. When I thought nobody was looking I practised climbing onto the roof of the boat. I could manage it, not very elegantly I admit, and the getting down was even more clumsy than the getting up, but I managed it. The knee twinged and was stiff but I reckoned that, if necessary, I could cope with the locks by myself. I was hoping to have some help along the River Nene so there would be some practice time and some more recovery time. The days were passing rapidly. It was the beginning of August and if I didn't set off for the canals soon, autumn and winter would be here and I never would move away. I did want to go, really I wanted to go. I think.

By Thursday afternoon I could find no more valid excuses for staying put and I was ready to leave. Eric strolled along to say goodbye and we stood watching the anglers along the bank. The schools were on holiday so it was mainly boys fishing, interspersed with a few girls, in a cut downwind from pungent scents of the pump out station. I wondered why they didn't move a few hundred yards downriver to the sweeter smelling, open countryside, out of the way of moored boats but they told me it was all to do with cost. It is free to fish between the bridges at either end of Ely outside of this area a licence is needed.

'Have you noticed if the leaks from the willow trees have harmed your paintwork?' asked Eric.

'I didn't know willow trees leaked,' I replied.

'Didn't you?' he sounded surprised at my ignorance, 'It's especially bad at this time of the year, it's the sap it drips on the roof and it damages the paintwork. That's why they call them weeping willows; they weep sap all over the place'

'Well you learn something new every day,' I said. I looked upwards and indeed I could feel the drips on my face. 'Yes, you're right, do you know it's the first time I've noticed it.' I moved to the boat and looked to see if I could see any sign of smears and marks on the paintwork. There were a few. I rubbed at them with my sleeve and they came off. I stood under the willow trees looking upwards. The drips become more persistent. 'That's rain,' I said.

Eric grinned, gave me a farewell wave and walked away.

I untied the boat, and pushed off from the bank but when I moved off I didn't do it very efficiently and my stern swung too close to the boys fishing in the cut. The fishing line of one of the lads caught in my propeller and he yelled at me. The rest of the fishing lads and lasses joined in and I immediately put the boat into neutral to stop the rest of the line ravelling around the propeller. The noise of the boys' shouting attracted the attention of the lad's Dad who emerged from beneath the railway bridge at a canter. He joined in the shouting, yelling that I'd just taken a brand new rod with me, a birthday present for the boy, and I must stop immediately. The boat was still in neutral and floating with the current. Looking behind I couldn't see any rod and there was nowhere to stop, so I moved very slowly forward intending to pull in after the bridge. The shouts from the bank were becoming more aggressive and the Dad was threatening me with grievous bodily harm and the complete annihilation of my boat. I threw back a bit of choice language and decided, in the interests of my safety, to move on a bit further before I stopped.

As a getaway vehicle a narrow boat leaves a lot to be desired, especially a narrow boat slowed down by a fishing line tangled in the propeller. I moved slowly along the river, Dad trotted along the bank spouting a stream of invective against me in particular and boaters in general. He was joined by his lad and a couple of mates. The threats from the bank increased in volume and ferocity. Secure in the knowledge that I was safe in the middle of the river I verbally retaliated. Later on, thinking about the exchange of words I recall that the really bad language came from my boat. The bankside contingent may have been threatening violence but they were mostly threatening it with words of more than four letters, on the other hand my verbal retaliations were using a limited vocabulary consisting words of one syllable.

Fortunately the Ouse is wide and long and eventually they got fed-up with the pointless pursuit of a boat they couldn't get near and they turned back towards Ely. I carried on to the first stopping place which was at Queen Adelaide, about three miles downriver. I grovelled in the weed hatch and found a length of fishing line wrapped around the propeller. I pulled on it expecting to find a rod attached to the line and maybe a boy attached to the rod. There was no sign of a rod, or a boy, just a long length of line which took an age to unravel.

I was glad to get out of range of the irate fisher folk but I did feel guilty because it was my fault and it was only a young boy whose line I had destroyed. I called Maureen and asked if she could go along to the fishing spot and speak to the boy (trying to avoid the father) and find out what damage I had actually done.

She texted me a short time later: '*His Dad says it was a new rod worth £100 and you've got to pay for it. I asked for their name and address but they can't read or write so couldn't put it down for me, somebody else is going to come and give me it. Don't pay, they're Pikies if they have a rod worth 100 quid it's because they nicked it.*'

Her second text came in twenty minutes later '*A woman in a pink woollen jumper that spent too long in the boil wash has just come with the address she said they want £7. I told her about your bad leg and she said if they'd known you were a cripple they wouldn't have kicked up so much fuss.*'

When I reached Outwell I put £10 in an envelope, included a florid letter of apology and posted it off safe in the knowledge that I wouldn't be back in Ely for a long time and wouldn't have to face another confrontation.

Two days later I returned to Ely. I'd left my keys in the lock of the pump-out station and a message reached me by a circuitous route that a passing boater had left them inside the pump-out for me to collect. With my hat pulled low and my collar pulled high I ploughed through the anglers and found a friendly boater who lent me keys to get into the pump-out station and collect mine. I hoped I wouldn't be recognised by any of the Lads or their Dads. I retrieved the keys and beat a hasty retreat.

Ely to Oundle

After I'd unravelled the fishing line from my propeller I travelled the intensely boring stretch of the Great Ouse between Ely and Littleport. There is a brief excitement at the presence of a large warehouse at Queen Adelaide, when that has crawled past there is nothing else to see. The river is dead straight and the banks are featureless. In the far distance there is a bridge that never gets any nearer. The Great Ouse is usually crammed with bird-life but this stretch seems to be devoid of any living thing, no birds or ducks or geese or swans, no cattle or sheep grazing the banks. The cables of the electrified railway run alongside the river but no train passes by. Grey clouds sink lower over grey water and it starts to drizzle. After a monotonous two hours I stop at The Ship Inn where my son and his girlfriend join me for yet another final farewell drink and a Bon Voyage dinner. I think I have done more farewell performances than Frank Sinatra.

The following morning I ring to check at what times the tides would be high enough to allow me to go through the lock at Denver onto the brief tidal stretch of river to join the Middle Levels at Salters Lode. I was told to arrive about 12pm, no need to book a slot just turn up and go through.

The morning was bright but I could see clouds gathering in the distance. Due to the limitless view of the wide skies of the Fens the weather never takes you by surprise. You can see it coming for miles. Bulbous black clouds heavy with rain head towards me. Being an optimist I think I will arrive at my destination before they reach me so I don't bother putting on my not very waterproof waterproofs or trying to locate my umbrella. The clouds are travelling faster than I have estimated. An hour short of Denver the black clouds catch up with me and sling a goodly portion of the North Sea down the back of my neck. One problem about being a single handed boater is that once up on the back of the boat it is difficult to go and get extra pieces of clothing and equipment especially if you can't remember where you left them. At this point the Great Ouse is so wide and straight that I could probably have gone into the cabin and cooked and eaten a three course meal and be doing the washing up before I hit the bank but I didn't have the confidence to leave the tiller to its own devices and go in search of waterproofs so I brazened it out. By the time I got to a mooring space I was drenched and cold. I tied up the boat and removed all the soggy bits of clothing, got a quick hot shower, dry clothes and drank a coffee. The rain had now stopped so I untied the boat and went on my way.

I had been told to arrive at Denver Lock around 12pm and it was now 12.30pm. There was a grump on duty.

'You're late,' he said.

'Have I missed the tide?' I asked.

'No,' he said, 'but 'it's a relief man on at Salters Lode and he won't want to be hanging around waiting for you, he'll be wanting his lunch.' With that he stomped off. I clambered off the boat, grovelling my way through all the goose shit that lay knee deep on the landing stage and tied up the boat wondering what to do next.

The grump came back. 'You're lucky, he'll let you through.' So I went into the huge lock and the gates clanged down and the water came up and the gates clanged open and I went on my way across the half mile tidal stretch between the Great Ouse and the turn onto the Middle Levels.

I nearly turned into the next lock, at Salters Lode, by aiming at a drunken black and white cross on a post. Unfortunately I was trying to turn too early and that would have meant I would have landed on a sand bank and probably have to sit on it for six hours until the tide turned and re-floated me. At the last minute I heard yells from the bank and saw the lock keeper gesticulating wildly for me to turn further on. 'Aim at the tyres!' he yelled. So I aimed at the bank of tyres that were fixed to the side of the wall at the entrance to the lock and managed to ping the boat neatly into the proper turning not the one that had just appeared to me to be the proper turning. I really must get my eyes tested.

'Didn't the bloke at Denver give you instructions where to turn?' asked the Salters Lode lock-keeper.

'No he bloody well didn't.' The grump must have decided that as I'd delayed everybody's lunch I deserved to spend the afternoon on a sand bank waiting for the tide to turn.

I continued on to the village of Upwell and moored

there for the night and the next morning I set off early so I could get to March in good time because I wanted to stop at Fox's Marina and get a mechanic to look at my batteries. They were not charging properly and I wanted to know why. I wondered if six weeks moored up with very little input from the engine had meant that they had run too low and therefore weren't taking a charge.

I called ahead to Marston lock and a nice lady said she would be there to help me through. She opened the lock gate when she saw me approaching and as I went in there was an almighty clunk and the boat came to an abrupt halt. I switched off the engine and leaned over to see what had happened. The chain that is attached to the side of the lock plus a few tons of blanket weed had wrapped themselves around my propeller. That was not good news. I got into the weed hatch and freed the few tons of blanket weed but the propeller remained well and truely entangled with the lock-side chain. The nice lady's husband and son came out and armed with a metal cutter eventually managed to cut the heavy chain and freed me. I left the lock apologising profusely for being such a complete idiot as to get tangled up in the chains on the side of the lock.

It was only when I was halfway to March that it dawned on me that I hadn't done anything wrong. I couldn't have. However badly I'd come into the lock it shouldn't have been possible to get tangled in the chains. I was the first one through the lock that day and overnight there had been a huge build-up of blanket weed which had wrapped itself around the chains. The turbulence created by gates opening and my propellers churning had forced the weed to float and in doing so had lifted the chain allowing it to catch around my propeller. I'm so used to doing everything wrong that my automatic reaction is to take the blame and apologise. I felt rather pleased that for once I was blameless but I did worry about the damage that may have been done to the rudder as my steering seemed even more erratic than usual.

I went uneventfully into March to get my batteries tested and re-charged. I was hoping that a good blast from a strong charger would cure the problems. A new bank of good quality batteries is very expensive and I was praying they weren't defunct.

I have attempted to adapt my life-style to the boat rather than adapt the boat to my lifestyle. If asked why I explain that I am living on a boat and espousing the simple life and I try to live as simply as possible in the most eco-friendly manner possible. The truth is that I don't want to spend lots of money on equipment and I am mechanically incompetent so probably wouldn't know how to install or operate said equipment. If a fault can't be cured by a squirt of WD40 or a few metres of gaffer tape then I have to revert to the third item in my toolbox, my cheque book. Even if I can see what needs doing I always fall at the first hurdle which is, 'getting the screws undone.' All work whether it be for boats or cars or domestic plumbing has been carried out by a large man who does strength training five times a week. A screw tightened by a professional with electric tools can never be undone by a lone woman with a manual screwdriver even with the help of an entire can of WD40. It is one of the unalterable laws of nature. It is why the professional has to be called in. It's not to do the repair or replacement that's the easy bit it's to loosen the damn screws. The professionals do the work and then replace the screws and tighten them with such ferocity that only superman can unscrew them and the cycle of reliance on workmen starts again. I can't even undo the diesel cap without help because some man with a larger and stronger grip than me has put it on too firmly. I try to do as I am told and check the oil in my gearbox but I can never undo the bolt that a mechanic tightened.

I live a simple life without any of the devices that some boaters feel to be essential but I can't be bothered to install or to have installed. The more bits of equipment one has the more things there are to go wrong. I don't need a gauge to tell me when I'm running out of diesel because I've got a wooden dipstick (or to be more precise I had a wooden dipstick until I let go when I was testing the levels and it fell into the tank). I don't want a water gauge because you have to go through the faff of calibrating them and if you put more load on the boat the calibrations are wrong and the gauge doesn't tell the truth. I know I'm running out of water when the taps start to cough when I turn them on. I know the gas is going to run out when I'm cooking a dinner for six and it's pouring with rain and a howling wind is blowing onto the bow where I have to stand to change the gas bottles. I know when the sewage tank needs a pump-out because the smell

227

permeates the entire length of the boat. I know the batteries need replenishing when the lights go out.

My electrical system depends on batteries that are charged by running the engine, I don't have a generator. The less electrical equipment I have the less often I need to run the engine to re-charge the batteries. Now I have removed the umbilical cord of the electric landline which I'd used in the marina over the winter I am mainly operating on 12 volt or using my inverter to convert to the more power hungry 240 volt. Hairdryers, electric kettles and electric heaters need a boost of energy to produce heat and trip my inverter immediately so they're not taking up room on board. I don't need a freezer. I'm only pootling around middle England I'm not sailing to the fjords of Scandinavia or to some unknown Tesco-free zone where fresh food is hard to come by so I don't need a stock of frozen food. When I lived in a house with mains electricity I only used the micro-wave to defrost food and as I haven't got a freezer I've nothing to defrost so I don't need a micro-wave. I hated a dishwasher when I had one, I seemed to spend more time cleaning the filters and stuffing chemicals in it than I did washing-up. I'd lived without a television for five years so there is no reason to have one now. I can go to a launderette rather than use the power/water hungry washing machine. The launderette is much more sociable anyway. My radio is battery operated. The thing I do need is my computer and I need it to have a good internet signal which I mostly get with a dongle. I can log into the systems of my customers in Spain and France and work from the boat. For my computer to work I need 240 volt power. If the power isn't there I can't work. I can run my engine to keep the inverter working but that isn't always practical, especially as the protocol is to only run engines and generators between the hours of 8am to 8pm to minimise disturbance to other boaters and river or canal side residents.

I stay in the marina at March for a couple of days and leave my batteries charging on a landline. Then the mechanic puts some fancy gadget on them and says the batteries are fully charged and functioning properly. I set off again happy that I will have power when I need it.

Then it's onwards to Peterborough, this time I'm waiting a couple of days for a friend to join me so I have a bit more time to look around. In most towns you can tell which famous people had connections with the area by looking at the names of the pubs. In St Ives there's the Oliver Cromwell, in Huntingdon the Lord Protector, in Northampton the Thomas a'Beckett and in Ely the Hereward. Cambridge has more famous people associated with it than it can be bothered to name pubs after. A relatively modern pub bears the name of the Isaac Newton but the rest of the famous residents and academics of Cambridge are left to languish in pub world obscurity.

In Peterborough the famous and influential don't have the ignominy of having public houses named after them they have the honour of giving their names to car parks. There's a Cavell (Edith went to school in Peterborough), Royce (partner of Rolls), Perkins (founder of Perkins Engines the largest employer in the city) and Clare (John, poet). John Clare was born in the village of Helpston about eight miles from Peterborough and lived for some time in Glinton again not quite in Peterborough but probably near enough if you have a large shopping centre with more car parks than famous inhabitants.

There isn't a car park named after Peterborough's most famous resident possibly because she never lived here when alive she has only been a resident since her death. Catherine of Aragon is buried in Peterborough Cathedral. She was exiled to Buckden Towers near Huntingdon then moved to Kimbolton Castle, about twenty miles south west of Peterborough, where she died. In 1536 she was buried in Peterborough Cathedral. Fifty years later her remains were joined by those of Mary Queen of Scots whose body was brought from the scene of her execution at Fotheringay Castle and was buried, 'with great solemnity,' on the instructions of Elizabeth 1. They only lay on opposite sides of the nave for twenty five years then James 1 had the remains of his mother Mary moved to the more prestigious setting of Westminster Abbey. Catherine was left as the solitary queen in this quiet and unpretentious cathedral. Each year on 27th January there is a commemorative service for Catherine of Aragon and around this date the cathedral organises a three-day Tudor festival.

When I visited the cathedral there were two simple posies of flowers laid on Catherine's grave. When I was in Fotheringay there had been flowers tied to the railings around the mound on which Mary Queen of Scots had been beheaded and on the ground there was a rose, dead and dehydrated but still with a tartan ribbon tied around it. I found these simple tributes to long gone queens, both casualties of the Tudor power struggles, rather touching.

The friend joined me at Peterborough and off we went on our merry way, leaving lock gates open, leaving keys in locks and windlasses on lock sides. As we were leaving Warmington Lock she meant to throw me the centre rope but somehow it dropped in the river. 'Not a problem,' I said starting to head off along the gunwale to fish it out of the water. I wasn't worried about the rope getting tangled in the propeller because this time I had made sure I got a rope that wasn't long enough to wind around it if it dropped in the river. Then I clunk to a halt. Well all I can think is that the woman in the chandlers didn't measure the rope correctly or the rope had stretched or my boat had shrunk because for the second time in my short boating career I'd ground to a halt due to my centre rope being well and truly wrapped around the propeller. At least this time I knew what to do. I got out the bread knife, rolled up my sleeves and squeezed down into the weed hatch to free the rope. The boat drifted diagonally across the river blocking navigation but luckily the Nene is a quiet river and there was nothing out navigating. Then the breeze gently moved the bow across and I was wedged to the side of a field where a line of curious calves came to watch my exertions. They stood motionless staring at me with an unblinking concentration. To get a centre rope caught in the propeller once is misfortunate to get a centre rope caught twice is carelessness. I'm not going to admit to anybody that it's happened to me.

We moored at Fotheringay my friend left and my daughter and son and their respective partners join me because it is my birthday. We plan to have a BBQ on the riverbank. It poured down with rain but we're British so undeterred we carry on huddled in raincoats, grilling meat under the shelter of umbrellas. Then having eaten our soggy burgers and steaks we get back on the boat, light the fire, finish the wine and gently steam.

The next morning the skies have cleared and it was a bright and warm August day. The sun shone on the four arches of the eighteenth century bridge giving the pale stone a mellow hue. The river was flat and placid and we could look down into the water and see the reeds and the fish swimming amongst them. The sheep and their fat lambs grazed in the field next to us. It was a perfect summer morning and we had a leisurely breakfast on the banks of the river. I had booked into Oundle Marina because I wanted a mechanic to check the connections to the batteries, despite being told they were charging properly I am still having problems with the inverter. When I switched the inverter on to allow me to use the 240 volt system it stayed on for a few minutes then tripped, which meant I can't use the computer. That's serious, no computer, no work, no money.

Tim had looked at the map to see how far it is to Oundle and realised we were going to be passing by

Aston and Aston is the home of the World Conker Championships which are held there every year in October. They were originally held on the village green in front of the pub until the competition grew too large for that area and had to be moved to a distant field. The previous year he had been sold a raffle ticket by a friend who was competing and he had won the first prize of a painting. So he rang the organiser and we arranged to meet her in the pub for the painting to be handed over. We knew we had plenty of time to meet her and have Sunday lunch, it was only about three hours to Oundle.

The boys decided to have a swim before we set off but they didn't stay in the water for long because the river was colder than they expected. Once they were back, shivering, on dry land we were off upriver. We moored in the cut just beyond Aston Lock and walked across fields and uphill to the Chequered Skipper pub in Aston where we met the Conker Championship organisers. We all admired the painting of cows in a field by the river and spent longer in the pub at Aston than we had planned. Not a problem though, we'd still got plenty of time to walk back down the hill to the boat and get to Oundle Marina before it closed. Well we would have if Tim hadn't decided to try out the satnav on his new phone. Alex, Jo and I went one way, Clare and Tim decided that they would go the way the satnav directed because it was sure to be much quicker. We three got back to the boat and waited for the other two, and waited and waited. Then we heard Clare calling, she was on the other side of the river knee deep in nettles. It was obvious there was no way through unless they fancied another swim. So they retraced their steps and eventually arrived back at the boat hot and bothered, covered in nettle rash and not in the best of moods.

So that is why the plan to get into Oundle Marina went astray. The marina closed at 5pm and it was 6pm before we arrived so I moored on the bank outside Oundle Cruising Club and we called a taxi to take my crew back to their car in Fotheringay. It was only respectful that as I was moored outside their club I should go in for a drink or three. In retrospect it could be said that by that chance mooring outside the club I had landed on my feet although it may be more anatomically correct to say I'd landed on my bum, and my bum was on a bar stool. But I didn't know that at the time I thought I was just spending a pleasant evening with chatty strangers before getting my problem with the batteries sorted and continuing on my way upriver and onto the canal system.

Stranded

The Plan was that I would spend a couple of days getting the battery problem resolved then move off up the Nene towards Northampton. A friend would join me at the weekend and we would get through the seventeen locks of the Northampton Arm then turn left and I'd head off towards London with the tentative plan of staying around the Leighton Buzzard area for the winter. But as I have often said before plans don't go to plan and stuff happens.

On Monday morning I called the hospital to chase up an appointment for a scan and found that it had been arranged for that afternoon. The paperwork had been sent to my old address because although the doctors had my friends address the hospital didn't. My fault, I shouldn't have expected joined up thinking between the doctors and the hospital. I left Oundle straight away and managed to get there in time for the appointment and stayed overnight with friends in Cambridge.

On Tuesday I arrived back and went into Oundle Marina and apologised about my non-arrival on Sunday and my disappearance on Monday and arranged for my batteries to be checked.

On Wednesday I left the boat walked one hundred yards and my leg collapsed in a sea of pain. For no apparent reason its state had returned to the day of the injury. I crawled back to the boat took the painkillers and lay down feeling exceedingly sorry for myself.

On Thursday the results of the scan came through

and I found out that I had to have an operation to remove my gall bladder. My leg was still in immobilised agony and my stomach pains were getting gradually worse.

On Friday the heavens opened and it rained torrentially all day.

On Saturday I put the blue leg brace back on, took the painkillers, got the crutches out of the engine room and made my way up to the clubhouse. There I found sympathy, help and alcohol and I was very grateful for all three.

On Sunday the Environment Agency posted Strong Stream warnings and closed the river to traffic so I wasn't going anywhere even if the useless leg, dodgy stomach and mal-functioning batteries allowed it.

The river remained closed for over a week. I was on the riverbank alongside a couple on a narrow boat and three couples on river cruisers, a small stranded community, friendly and helpful to a woman having difficulty walking. If the river had not been closed I would have had crew to help me progress and I think I would have risked moving even with the encased and painful knee, but the weather prevented me from having to make a decision and I was grateful for that, decisions were becoming as painful as the knee. I just rested the leg, read books and talked to my neighbours and a couple of anglers who were spending most days fishing from the bank alongside the boats. A constant topic of conversation amongst the anglers was bait. It appears bait is a complex and ever fascinating subject to anglers. I thought fish ate anything, I've sat here and watched them jump for insects and chase smaller fish and gather around when I throw bread out for the ducks, I've seen them nibbling at weed and fighting over the leftovers I've thrown overboard. I wasn't aware that they had discerning palates.

'Chub like cheese,' number one fisherman says.

'I've been told that Perch like jelly babies,' number two fisherman says, 'So I'm trying out jelly babies.'

'Do the Perch have a colour preference, I always like the black ones, do they bite the heads off first?' I ask.

'Don't know,' he says, 'I haven't had a bite yet.'

Ten minutes later he catches a duck. Fish may not like jelly babies but mallards appear to be quite partial to them. The fisherman hauls the duck in gently, picks it out the water, and the duck sits patiently on his knee as he spends the next twenty minutes removing the hook from its mouth. Once released the duck paddles away repeatedly dipping his head in the water and shaking it vigorously.

By Wednesday the rain had stopped falling and we all waited for the powers that be at the Environment Agency to proclaim that the river is safe to travel on. I went hopefully to bed on the Thursday night. At 3am I was woken by a loud crash and thought about getting out of bed to investigate, changed my mind pulled up the duvet, turned over and nearly fell out of bed. The boat was listing heavily. I got up hobbled down the corridor and discovered that the crash was my vase of flowers falling off the shelf. The cupboard doors on the bankside of the boat were wide open, the floor leaned to the left. I thought the boat was sinking.

My sleep befuddled brain couldn't work out why. Had I been holed during the night? Was water rushing into the bilges? Was I about to be sent to the depths of the River Nene? I got off the boat. I got back on the boat and got a torch and a dressing gown. It was a black night with a strong but mild wind and smatterings of rain. I shone the torch along the bow of the boat, it didn't appear to have been struck by an ice-berg. The ropes had ply in them and weren't pulling me over. I shone the torch along the riverbank, the river had dropped dramatically during the night and a slime of mud glistened above the water line. The boat was grounded along one side. I tried standing on the bank and pushing it off but that didn't work. The other four boats along the bank were floating and their occupants were most likely sleeping peacefully. I wondered what I'd do if I couldn't move the boat. I didn't fancy being on board if it was sinking and I didn't fancy hanging around on the bankside until dawn when I could get some help. The wind sloughed through the trees, yellow lights on the roadside flickered behind disturbed leaves, a coot on the marina screeched. I stood there indecisively.

A gust of wind blew droplets from the willow trees overhanging the bank the wet splatter on my face stirred me into action and I climbed painfully onto the back of the boat, took the boat pole and pushed and pushed and eventually felt the pole moving. I couldn't tell if it was the boat moving or the pole sinking into the mud of the bank. I'd managed to place the torch so

238

it only dazzled me and didn't illuminate anything of any use. Then the boat rocked and we were free and floating. I went back inside, removed my soggy slippers and my wet dressing gown and got back into my once more level bed but I didn't get back to sleep until it was time to get up.

By the time the river was re-opened for navigation my potential crew had returned to work and I was definitely not going to be able to manage any locks by myself. Once more I was stranded on a riverbank only this time I was a long hobble from the shops and didn't have friends and relatives nearby to pop over and help.

The Marina managed to find me a mooring for a few weeks which gave me a breathing space but they had strict rules about how long I was allowed to live on board. Most marinas are non-residential and have rules about how many days that owners are allowed to stay overnight on their boats. Other marinas have a limited amount of residential berths only a very few are totally residential. There are rules about council tax if a boat is lived in and stays in the same place for a certain length of time. Each district council varies both the regulations and how stringently they are applied. Ultimately it is the marine owner who is responsible if the boat owner does not pay the council tax due, hence their reluctance to have live-aboards on site. Canal and River Trust have some residential moorings on the canals. When applying for a licence Canal and River Trust states clearly that a boat has to have a home-base or to be continuous cruising. Their definition of continuous cruising is 'the boat travels widely around the waterway network without staying in any one place for more than fourteen days'. Rules are rules and rules are broken, that's what they're there for. Marina owners decide not to notice people living on board, councils can't be bothered to check on sites. Continuous cruisers stay put or move backwards and forwards along a couple of miles of canal. If boaters have work or children at school or simply have a social life in one area it isn't feasible to move forever onwards. In theory they should have a residential mooring but residential moorings are in short supply. In some regions not only are they hard to come by they are also very expensive. In London a residential mooring in a good area could cost in the region of £7,000 to £9,000 per annum so it is little wonder that people aren't able to afford them. The boaters who move backwards and forwards along a short stretch of canal are known as bridge hoppers. The Brian and Janets of the boating world, the 'Living the Dream' couples in their polished boats hate the bridge hoppers, they consider them only one rung on the ladder above hire boaters. They moan about them taking space at popular points, cluttering the towpath and having scruffy boats. Canal and River Trust occasionally prosecute boaters when they flout the regulations too blatantly. It is difficult to know how many of the boats on the canal system are fully residential yet don't have a residential mooring because these are the people without permanent addresses, who don't get census forms who don't have television licences and are not registered for tax. Some live an alternate, hand to mouth way of life getting bits of work here and there, producing craft, playing music living a life that keeps them well under the radar of the state. A family I met had lived this kind of life for many years and had survived on cash in hand jobs painting boats. They didn't pay tax but always made sure they paid their Canal and River Trust licence fees. They didn't have a bank account so saved the money for the licence in a tin and then took hundreds of pounds in cash into the Canal and River Trust office in Milton Keynes. Canal and River Trust didn't like this method of payment they prefer direct debits and bank transfers but for the time being they had to accept it.

I had been planning to continuous cruise but my plans hadn't worked out. My journey so far could be better described as continuous stopping rather than continuous cruising. I had got permission from the Environment Agency to stay put in St Ives until I was able to manage the boat so I hadn't broken any rules when I was there. I had bought a Gold Licence which meant I could cruise on both the rivers which are managed by the Environment Agency and the canals which are managed by Canal and River Trust. Gold licences cost over £1,000 and are not refundable. As I'd never reached the canal system and it didn't look as if I was going to I could have saved myself money and bought a licence for the Nene and Great Ouse which cost £700. I could have spent that £300 wisely on designer crutches or medicinal red wine.

Once I'd decided not to continue onwards I moved onto a temporary berth in the marina but it was on a far bank and a ten minute hobble to the gate. My gall bladder was causing me a lot of pain, especially in the evening. I was told that if I had another severe attack I should call an ambulance and go to hospital. The problem was that I was locked into the marina at night and there was nobody else around as it was not a residential site. If I had to call an ambulance I had no idea how I would get to the gate to let them in. For the first time since I had bought the boat I felt vulnerable and alone.

Yet in the middle of this there is joy. My son and his girlfriend got married. One of the bankside anglers gave me a lift to the train station and I spent a delightful weekend being the mother of the groom. After a few glasses of champagne I cast aside the crutches and danced, ate all the things that would cause my gall bladder to complain and had a totally wonderful time. I paid heavily for my excesses; the next few days were exceedingly painful.

Back at the boat, after a period of post-wedding recovery, I set about looking for a mooring. The denizens of the cruising club sprang into action and gave me telephone numbers and took me to look at sites and bullied one site manager to move a few boats around so that they had space for me. Another member sourced me a reliable second hand car. By the end of September I had a mooring for the winter on a riverbank with a beautiful view across the fields to the church at Stoke Doyle. I had transport. I was amidst a friendly and helpful community and I felt safe. I knew if I was ill I would have help. The best bit of boating is definitely the stopping.

Oundle

So this is where the squires of Northamptonshire lurk. Squire-like persons might not have been evident in Northampton or Wellingborough or Corby but they are out in force in Oundle. They can be seen in Cotton's shoe shop trying on brogues. They are in the pet shop buying squeaky toys for their Labradors. They are in Jacs waiting for their wives to try on smart dresses. They are having a gin and tonic in the bar of the Talbot Hotel. They're buying vintage claret in Amps wine shop. They're visiting their children, pupils at Oundle School, and treating them to cakes in one of the coffee shops. They're wearing green tweed jackets with a thin red check that are the uniform for the middle classes when they are attending National Hunt meetings and point to points. Their well-modulated voices can be heard ordering venison and artisan cheeses from the stalls at the monthly farmer's market.

If I can describe Northamptonshire as nice Oundle must be the nicest town in Northamptonshire. Its old mellow stone houses laze in the autumn sunshine, a plethora of wonky tiled roofs and crooked chimney pots rise above the Nene Valley. St Peter's Church stands at the highest point, its tall spire visible for miles around. The Old Town Hall, built in a Tudor style although not in Tudor times, stands in the middle of the Market Place. Oundle School dominates the town with solid honey stone buildings, some dating back to the early sixteenth century. During term time the smartly uniformed pupils of Oundle school swell the population of Oundle by twenty five per cent.

Sitting in Beans coffee shop on a Wednesday afternoon I watch the pupils from Oundle School walk past. Where are the fat kids? A recent survey said that nearly thirty per cent of children and young adults in Northamptonshire are overweight or obese. Not at Oundle School they're not. These young people seem taller than the average youth of their age, are fit and healthy looking with little noticeable extra fat. I can't even see that there are many fat kids amongst the pupils of Prince William Secondary School, the state school on the edge of Oundle. To make up the obesity percentages there must be a school in the county where ninety per cent of the children are overweight. Maybe it's in Corby where the children going to school don't look as if they are the children of Northamptonshire squires.

Oundle School pupils are confident, neat and polite and only ever walk around in pairs. They never block the pavements or cause problems in the shops. Most of the girls have long blonde hair that can be flicked away from the face. Does the school have a blonde quota for its female pupils? Whether blond, brunette or red head flickable hair for the girls, hair that is glossy and touches the shoulder blades is as much part of the uniform as the flowing pin striped trousers and boxy jackets that they wear. For the boys it's a neat short back and sides, no scruffy hair falling to the shoulders, no spikey quiffs, not a trace of punk. The uniformity of the pupils goes beyond the wearing of the uniforms and extends to what must be a self-imposed uniform of hair and attitude. All the pupils carry their books clasped to their chests, never are the books carried in school bags even when the books are multitudinous and heavy. Is it part of the rules that books must not be put in bags or is it just a tradition that is never broken? There is not the customisation of the uniform that was noticeable at a school in Daventry. I was stuck in traffic watching the pupils leave and was entertaining myself counting the variety of ways in which a school tie could be worn. They were worn tight and short, long and loose, frayed, big knots, small knots, cut off ends everything but a conventional knotted tie. When I thought I'd seen all the possible ways of wearing a tie I transferred my attention to the variety of ways it was possible to wear the conventional pleated skirt that was also part of the uniform. At Oundle School every tie has a neat knot, every pupil conforms to the norm, presumably if they didn't Mummy and Daddy would be asked to remove them.

As I'm leaving the cafe a lone girl crosses the road she carries her books in a bag, she has short red curly hair and her bum looks big in her stripey trousers. She looks confident and couldn't care less that her appearance doesn't quite fit the standard of the rest of the school. Have I spotted the school's rebel?

I look up the list of famous Old Oundelians and amongst them is Richard Dawkins and Bruce Dickinson, the lead singer with the heavy metal band Iron Maiden, somehow I could imagine this school producing them both. I was surprised to see Arthur Marshall amongst the names, a very amusing broadcaster who I remembered listening to years ago. Then when I thought about it, it was not so much that Arthur Marshall went to Oundle School it was more that he went to school at all. I thought of him as forever elderly. There was only one famous old girl mentioned in the list, an actress I'd never heard of. I wonder what the girls of Oundle School do when they leave. Marry squires?

I was showing a friend around Oundle. We meandered around in and out of the shops, stopped for a coffee, strolled down the streets passed the antique shops. As we rounded another corner into another street of stone built cottages she said, 'After a while all these buildings built of the same stone become tedious.'

I suppose Oundle is a bit samey. It's not just the pale stone of the buildings that flank the streets or the Oundle School pupils in their uniforms but also the inhabitants, all clean and neat and respectable. But I like it. It has independent shops, good butchers and bakers, dress shops that I can't afford to shop in, coffee shops that aren't Starbucks. It has a wine shop that I can go into and drool. It has a weekly Thursday market and a monthly farmer's market. It's got a weekly Sunday cinema and music in the church. It's a small attractive market town. It's nice.

I didn't plan to be stopping here and wintering on the River Nene but I'm happy with the way things have turned out, I'm not sure I really wanted to be on a canal in the winter where there is a strong possibility of being frozen in, waterless with an overflowing toilet. Living on a river is much more interesting than living in a marina or on a canal. There is the variety of wildlife. On Saturdays and Sundays there are rowers on the river and the occasional passing boat to wave at. On the bankside there are chickens wandering about. The cockerels crow every morning and remind me of living in the Philippines were every other household owned a vocal fighting cock. In the fields beyond the bank are Herdwick sheep and Tamworth and Berkshire pigs, I am already getting fond of Elsie, the large Tamworth sow who lets me rub her bristly snout. In the skies above the bank the red kites cruise and their plaintive Fi Fi Fi cry is an ever present background sound. At night the bank is pitch black except when the moon is full and then it is light enough to walk in the fields without the aid of a torch. On clear nights the lack of ambient light means the stars are brilliant in the black sky. If I'm feeling lonely there are people to talk to or at weekends I can go to the local clubhouse. Mark, the Mechanical Magician, has found the fault with my batteries that the mechanics at two marinas had failed to find, it was some switchy thingy that needed replacing. Alan has replaced the starter motor in my central heating system.

The resident Man that Knows Everything came onto the boat and politely removed his shoes, two minutes later he had very soggy socks. I've had an intermittently wet carpet for over nine months now and it's getting worse and I can't work out where the water is coming from. I get a long lecture from the Man that

Knows Everything on the subject of boats and water. The précis version is that when living on a boat all water should be on the outside there should be none on the inside, water on the inside of boats is not good. After he's left I go to get paint from one of the cubby holes at the back of the boat and find it is sitting in inches of water. I bail out, mop up and then think maybe I ought to worry about all this water. He comes back and diagnoses a leak in the water pump and he gets a new pump and replaces it. He also fixed my leaky pipe and replaced the alternator and something else back there that stopped my boat working and he's unblocked my drain and he's sealed my sink. And he's told me in no uncertain terms that women shouldn't be allowed to live on boats because they are all mechanically inept and wouldn't know how to change an oil filter if their life depended on it. He says women haven't the brain capacity to operate anything more technically difficult than a tin opener or a washing machine and should steer well clear of anything with engines. He could be right.

I'll stay here until the spring and carefully plan next year's trip. Hopefully my operation will have been a success and my leg will have recovered and I will be fit and refreshed and be ready to carry on from where I left off.

I'm even looking forward to winter: to lighting the fire and letting casseroles simmer on the stove: to winter walks and to the silence and solitude of the riverbank: to getting the maps out and planning next year's journey. I'm more used to boat living now, I've got thermal curtains over the doors, I've sealed the draughts, I've bought (at great expense) a copper whirly thingy, formally known as an eco-fan which stands on top of the stove and circulates the warm air and goodwill along the length of the boat. I have even worked out how to keep the fire constantly alight. I have got thermal underwear and thick socks and fluffy slippers.

When I bought the boat there were six flowery porthole bungs in one of the lockers, I thought they looked odd and couldn't make out what they were for, so I slung them out. Now I wish I hadn't, they were meant as insulation for the porthole windows. At least I didn't get around to demolishing my cratch cover, it stops draughts and is a useful waterproof cover for coal and wood and I've stocked up with coal and wood and it is lying dry and accessible under the cratch cover.

So this year I should be all right and if yet another person asks if the boat is cold and damp in the winter I'll be able to say, 'Not at all it's toastie.' And anyway this winter can't possibly be as cold as last winter.

The Final Journey

It was five years later, five years almost to the day when I started to do a return journey from the Fens to Denver across the Middle Levels and onto Braunston.

It was a perfect September day, perfect for boating, warm and sunny with a light wind, exactly the same early placid autumnal weather we had had for that first trip.

I'd had to book the passage through the lock at Isleham because one of the gates was faulty and needed the Environment Agency to operate it. I drove in far too fast scraped the side of the lock and only stopped because I banged into the gate. 'Is this your first time on a boat?' asked the Environment Agency man.

It wasn't, of course, I'd been driving my boat around for the last five years only this time I was on the Fellow Traveller's boat. It handled differently to mine, it had precision steering and no brakes, that was my excuse anyway. It did make me wonder if I had been premature and harsh with my criticism of his boat handling skills when we'd first travelled together; it didn't seem an easy boat to control.

In August, Michael, the ex, the Fellow Traveller, had died. I was taking his boat back to the canal system to put it on brokerage. I had help moving the boat and we travelled faster towards the canal system than the two of us novices, on our newly acquired boats, did on that first journey travelling towards the Great Ouse. After all this time there was no steep learning curve to climb and I didn't have to stop for screaming matches with the Fellow Traveller.

The River Nene was beautiful and well behaved the weather was kind but it was a sad and poignant journey for me especially knowing how much Michael would have loved to be doing this himself. Despite the errors, the mishandling of the boats and all the shouting he had thoroughly enjoyed that first journey. We had both travelled hopefully into a new way of life. Now I felt a usurper on his boat. He should have been at the helm, listening to the call of the red kites, enthusing about the scenery, getting cross when the locks were full and he had to negotiate onto one of the short lock landings. He would have loved stopping at the riverside pubs or mooring at isolated spots and getting his camera out and photographing the sun setting over the river.

As we sailed along the Nene I had constant reminders of our first journey: the lock where my centre rope got entangled in the prop, the lock where he nearly went over the weir, where we met the Queen of The Nene. I remember we had fish and chips in that pub and a drink in that one where he moaned about the price of the beer and that one where we watched a game of skittles.

In spite of the perfect travelling conditions it was a relief to get to the destination and leave the boat with the brokers, for the weeks of watching our children take on the heart breaking task of clearing the boat of their fathers belongings, preparing it for sale and moving it had been painful. The boat sold quite quickly, it is a lovely boat and I hope its new owner loves it as much as Michael did.

Michael applied for a mooring in Cambridge, the list is long and for four years he watched his name climb slowly to the top. On the day of his funeral an email arrived saying his much awaited mooring was now available. We can imagine him saying, 'Bloody typical,' and having an endless rant about the irony of it. He did a good rant.

We scattered his ashes in the Cam alongside Jesus Green where he would have moored. We thought the ashes would have

251

come in an urn but they came in a sort of hoover bag. So we put them in a Co-op carrier bag and carted them through Cambridge, he often shopped at the Co-op so he wouldn't have minded that. At one point we nearly left his ashes behind in a pub, but it was a pub he liked so he wouldn't have minded that either. We poured the ashes into the Cam but didn't look to see which way the wind was blowing so his sister had grey ash all over her black coat. We imagined how he would have laughed at our shenanigans.

We'd lived in the village of Willingham when the children were growing up. Friends from the village planted a tree in their new community orchard in his memory. They chose a crab apple tree. He'd have laughed at that as well.

Lightning Source UK Ltd.
Milton Keynes UK
UKOW03f2012120217

294177UK00005B/285/P